ROBERT WELCH · HAND & MACHINE

HAND

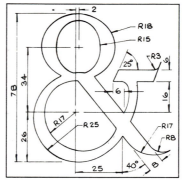

MACHINE

ROBERT WELCH
DESIGNER · SILVERSMITH

Copyright © 1986 Robert Welch

First edition 1986
Published by Robert Welch
The Mill Chipping Campden
Gloucestershire GL55 6DU

ISBN 0 951085 50 6

Designed by Pentagram
Typesetting by Filmcomposition England
Printed in Hong Kong
British Library
Cataloguing in Publication Data
Welch, Robert, 1929-
    Hand & Machine
    1 Metal-work 2 Design
    I Title
    739 NK6404

Contents

FOR PATRICIA

ACKNOWLEDGEMENTS

I would like to express my thanks and gratitude to the following for invaluable help and encouragement in the preparation of this book.

David Hillman of Pentagram for the concept and design of the book and his assistant designer, Amanda Bennett for endless patience and for coping with such a mass of material, not to mention the numerous changes, many when the book seemed to have reached a finalised design stage.

Alan Crawford who acted as consultant editor and who undertook this task when his own magnum opus on the life of C. R. Ashbee was in its final stages of completion. Roger Inman who read the texts and gave much valuable help and advice, and Lilias Foggin, my secretary, for great help with the typescripts.

John Limbrey who created reality out of so many ideas; a special thank you appears on page 200.

To the photographers, Enzo Ragazzini, David Cripps and Roger Stowell, who were responsible for most of the photographs, and finally Colin Forbes of Pentagram, New York, a special thank you for the confidence to produce this book.   ROBERT WELCH, 1985

ROBERT WELCH

1929	Born in Hereford
1936	Parents moved to Malvern, Worcestershire.
1946-55	Studied at Malvern School of Art, Birmingham College of Art and the Royal College of Art.
1954-55	Developed special interest in stainless steel.
55	Appointed consultant to Old Hall Tableware; set up a silversmithing workshop in the Mill, Chipping Campden, Gloucestershire.
1956	Exhibition at Foyle's Art Gallery – Silver and Stainless Steel.
1956	Visiting teacher, London Central School of Arts & Crafts, Department of Industrial Design.
1957	Tableware for S.S. ORIANA.
1958	John Limbrey joined Robert Welch's workshop.
1962	Alveston cutlery designed for Old Hall Tableware.
1962	First designs for cast iron.
1964	Exhibition of silver tableware at Heal's.
1965	First designs for Carl Prinz A.G., Western Germany.
1967	Exhibition of Industrial design and silverware at Heal's.
1969	Opened Robert Welch Studio Shop close to workshop in Chipping Campden.
1970	First deigns for cast iron cookware, H. E. Lauffer Inc., U.S.A.
1973	ROBERT WELCH: DESIGN IN A COTSWOLD WORKSHOP, published by Lund Humphries.
1975	First visit to India at the invitation of the All India Handicraft Board.
1979-80	Visit to Japan and first designs for Yamazaki.
1981-82	Yamazaki Serving Collection.
1984	Bronze casting, India, visit to establish programme.

PREFACE

In 1955 Robert Welch set up as a silversmith on the top floor of an old mill building at Chipping Campden in Gloucestershire. He was a young man on the look-out for work, and he slept on a little truckle bed in the corner of the workshop. Today, thirty years later, he still works there. He has received awards and honours, his work has been acquired by museums, and his designs have been manufactured all over the world. Other people would have courted success, moved to London perhaps. Robert Welch has chosen to stay where he is. Rootedness is part of his character, and he enjoys designing in a quiet, steady atmosphere.

The designs in this book are arranged under the twin headings of Hand and Machine. From the start, his work has included some designs for unique objects to be made in his own workshop, and others for industrial production. Now one will preponderate, now the other; but it is essential to the way he works that they should both be there. The title is neither glib nor argumentative. It simply reflects a two-handed process, one kind of work prompting and correcting the other. How fruitful the process has been, the rest of this book shows.   ALAN CRAWFORD

INTRODUCTION

I have in front of me an old sketch book which belonged to my mother, bound in brown leather, slightly padded, with the word 'Album' tooled on the centre of the cover. The first page is inscribed – 'To Dorothy Perkins, from Mum, Christmas 1915'.

I have known this sketch book since my childhood and from a very early age I wondered and marvelled at the skill and fine draughtsmanship of the drawings it contained. The illustrations run consecutively through the pages; indeed the book was used partially as a superior autograph album, with friends contributing carefully executed drawings as their own memento, interspersed with drawings by my mother; but soon after the middle of the 1920s she gave up drawing and painting altogether.

As a child I was allowed to add my own drawings to this fine book, but I felt this was sacrilege and was clearly overawed by the standard. My contribution was limited to several efforts only.

My mother attended Hereford Art School from 1914 to 1917, and to judge by the standard she achieved, she received an excellent training in drawing and painting under the Headmaster, Mr. Bainton, and her teachers, Miss Dudson and Miss Shaw. The sketch book contains many drawings executed by her contemporaries who were a very talented group of students; but with the Great War in progress and all the young male students in the Forces, the chances of pursuing art seriously were almost non-existent. Life at home was equally difficult; my Grandfather was a Welsh hill farmer who had fought in the Boer War, and his two sons, who might have been helping to run the farm, were away at the war; neither of them returned.

One of the most brilliant students at Hereford was Hilda Peplow, and she alone pursued a career in art by taking a job as a lithographic artist with a local firm. This was one area of creative work where an artistic training could be usefully employed no matter how difficult the economic situation and problems of commerce in wartime.

This, however, was not for my mother, and after painting a fine portrait of Hilda Peplow, she left Art School to do her bit for the war effort, taking a job at Hereford Munitions Factory at Rotherwas, a job not without considerable danger as the exploding of shells was not uncommon.

During her Art School days she subscribed to STUDIO magazine which at the time was still the most influential magazine concerned with the arts. It

Dorothy Welch, 1897-1982. Penelope.
Pencil drawing, size 180 mm x 140 mm,
from the Album of 1915.

covered all branches of art, including architecture, and one of the special features of this magazine was the design competition in which projects were suggested and the winning and commended entries were later published in the magazine. These competitions were frequently entered by students of Hereford Art School, but on some occasions were merely used as the inspiration for tackling an unusual problem. One example of this was a design for a table centrepiece, painted on silk with poppies and wheatsheaves swirling together in a gentle Art Nouveau design, which won for my mother the Hereford Art School Prize for 1914: a book on the Peak District.

I grew up in an environment where I did not actually see my mother draw or paint as she had given up these activities around the time of her marriage in 1925, but in a way, the fact that the house was full of canvas, watercolours and drawings, as well as an enticing pile of old STUDIO magazines, added a strange excitement to art for me.

I was frustrated when I tried to copy my mother's drawings – the subtlety eluded me, yet I tried desperately to produce work of the same calibre. As my mother ceased to produce her art I was not daunted as I might have been by a demonstration of her prowess had she continued to paint. Instead there was a finite collection of art, a complete monument of her achievement. Examples of her work were always before me to absorb, try to improve upon, or reject in whatever I chose to do. Even more important, there was never any criticism, only encouragement for my attempts at drawing and painting.

I was so imbued with the romance of an Art School that it was an obvious choice for me to enrol at Malvern School of Art as soon as I had left school; and despite the passing of thirty years the philosophy at Malvern in 1946 was almost the same as that at Hereford in 1915. In fact, in many ways my mother's background may have been more radical with the strong influence of STUDIO to supplement teaching. At Malvern, painting was the name of the game. Hours were spent on drawings from life and anatomy, but no matter how well one thought one drew, there was always someone making drawings which put one to shame. Usually, of course, it was the brilliant artist, Victor Moody, who would in a few deft strokes coax a miraculous interpretation of the model, which left one demoralised, rather than encouraged.

Both schools taught the values that were sound and timeless, yet undeniably narrow for those who

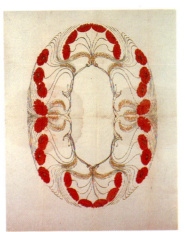

Dorothy Welch, 1897-1982. Wheatsheaves and Poppies. Painting on silk, size 660 mm x 540 mm. Hereford Art School Prize 1914.

did not aspire to painting; but in the 1940s, was there anything else one should have been thinking about?

Art schools were to do with art, and at Malvern, art was the Life Class and Anatomy, and who is to say, even today, that this was not the most excellent training, if not the most perfect introduction to design? But Malvern did offer students the opportunity to sample different disciplines, such as modelling from life and bookbinding, and there was also a weekly class for metalwork run by Miss Ballard, who had studied at Birmingham under Bernard Cuzner. It was with her encouragement that I decided to embark on a career as a silversmith. On the 18th of July, 1950, I got a letter from the Director of Education for Worcestershire County Council, which read – "Dear Mr. Welch, I have been asked by the County Treasurer to forward you a cheque for one pound ten shillings in respect of the Charlotte Jacob Prize for Silversmithing for the 1949-50 session at Malvern Art School."

Armed with this prize I left Malvern to begin my studies in silversmithing in earnest, under Ralph Baxendale and Cyril Shiner, at Birmingham College of Art. Here the emphasis was all on silversmithing as a craft, history and design; but at the time it seemed quite impossible to contemplate being able to earn one's living practising this craft. The future looked very bleak indeed, and everyone's thoughts turned towards teaching as a career. Purchase tax was chargeable on silver at over 100% and England was still in post-war depression, with shortages of all kinds, ration books still in use, and industry working for export orders with many materials only available on licence.

Two years later, when I had moved to the Royal College of Art, I decided that I must pursue the possibility of designing for industrial production, an area which I found very challenging, and in my last year I specialised exclusively in stainless steel production design.

Scandinavia loomed large as an influence in the mid-'50s; the philosophy of the Scandinavians, so popular at that time, designing simple, everyday objects that were functional and beautiful and which most people could afford, greatly appealed to me. I was, and remain, committed to this ideal and since the '50s I have endeavoured to pursue this aim along with the craft of silverwork.

The challenge of the two activities has always proved stimulating – silver, with its traditional background, frequently made as a unique piece or in small batches, is intrinsically valuable, often cared for lovingly and destined to be an heirloom for generations to come. Whereas, the manufactured article can embrace advanced technology, create and maintain jobs, be improved by the continual search for greater efficiency. The volume of production can be enormous and the high capital investment for tooling can result in objects which are of great beauty being manufactured at modest prices.

It has long been my conviction that each area can enrich the other to a very important degree. With silver design one has 'carte blanche', anything can be made, and there is a danger of degenerating into self-indulgence; but then the discipline of the dual background comes to the rescue, helping to establish the appropriate functional form and fine detailing. On the other hand, industrial products may be designed to embody a warmth of feeling and tactility which transcends the impersonalised methods of production; and the silver workshop can become the laboratory of design and research for industrial forms.

I believe that it is possible to blend the best of these two worlds, the old and the new, the unique and the multiple, hand and machine, to the mutual advantage of each other.   ROBERT WELCH

Dorothy Welch, 1897-1982. Portrait of Hilda Peplow. Oils on Canvas 1917, size 320 mm x 210 mm.

In the Spring of 1964 I had a long conversation with Rolf Falk, the buyer of Heal's, during which we discussed the problem of domestic silverware, and finally we came to the conclusion that if it were possible to sell modern tableware in stainless steel then it should be possible to sell a range of modern silverware, using hand and machine methods.

We decided to embark upon this project, and I undertook to design and make in my workshop a collection of pieces that would be loosely unified by a family resemblance to each other, and to do my best to make these pieces at prices which would enable Heal's to add on their required mark up and still be at a sensible price for their customers.

For his part, Rolf Falk undertook to acquire a pair of fine glass showcases with good safe locks, print a catalogue and arrange to have a small party on the day of the launching of the collection.

Sir Gordon Russell opened the evening with an informal speech and I felt immense gratitude towards him for travelling to London specially for this occasion. Looking back now I can see that his long and friendly association with Heal's matched closely his keen interest in Campden and its crafts. Both these aspects made the whole subject close to his heart.

Pencil and wash drawing for Cream Jug.

The late Gunnar Bratveld, the editor of MOBILIA magazine, and Professor Ole Wancher, both of Copenhagen, were at Heal's on a visit, gathering material for an article to appear in MOBILIA later that year. They attended the party and afterwards, during a visit to Gordon Russell's factory at Broadway, they called at my workshop and kindly recorded their impressions of the visit in an entertaining and well illustrated diary of events covering this, which formed the basis of the article later published in MOBILIA.

The Heal's range of silver may not have been of any financial consequence to the store itself, except perhaps that it did attract a lot of publicity, and Harold Wilson as Prime Minister, took a number of pieces to Russia as Government gifts to the leaders, Mr. Kosygin and Mr. Mikoyan, and continued to use the collection for these purposes on various official visits thereafter.

For me, personally, the Heal's collection was of great importance – it established the style of a collection of silver that we make in the workshop to this day, and even in 1983 the British Embassy in Manila was largely equipped with table silver that was first shown at Heal's in 1965. By the end of the 1960s the sale of silver in Heal's had declined sharply and the close relationship between us gradually ceased; but

Pencil and wash drawing for Cream Jug.

the great effort that was expended in gathering the collection together was not wasted. At a further exhibition held at Heal's in 1967, I showed not only silver, but a collection of products manufactured to my designs by a variety of companies as well, and concurrently an identical exhibition opened in Skjalm Petersen's shop in Copenhagen.

I could see that the idea of mixing domestic silver and product designs together was a good one, and it was this idea which was the germ of the Studio Shop which I opened in Chipping Campden in 1969; that, in its turn, has increased the sales of domestic silver.

Of all the ingredients required for this mixture, domestic silverware was, and remains, of the greatest importance for me. It is an interesting point that all aspiring silversmiths begin by a careful consideration of single everyday objects, the type of silver that one naturally relates to and naturally wishes to make. This is the type of silver that the English silversmiths have always excelled at, unselfconscious, functional, usually simple and forthright in conception.

Yet, even though such silver seems so important at the beginning of one's introduction to the craft, when it comes to earning one's living as a professional craftsman, this is the very area which proves most

Teapot, handle bound with plastic, 1953.

difficult to pursue with adequate financial returns. The silversmith, probably more than any other craftsman, relies upon commissioned work, which, by its commemorative nature, usually lifts the piece away from the very qualities that are so important in domestic silver. This was a problem that I soon became aware of during the early days of my workshop and this is why the Heal's silver collection has seemed so important to me.

Condiment set in amethyst glass with silver mounts, 1953.

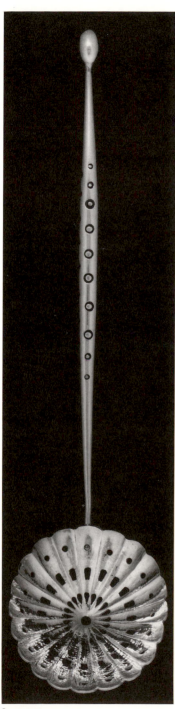

BERGEN, NORWAY 1953

In the summer of 1953 I was one of a group of Design students from the Royal College and from Kingston College of Art who were invited to work for a few weeks in various factories in Bergen.

The only silversmith, I worked with Theodore Olsen, a factory that specialised in enamelware, and I made two pieces. One of them was a silver vase with deeply cut vertical lines, which were to have been covered with translucent enamel, but time ran out.

At the end of the visit Theodore Olsen offered me a job as a designer and Bergen Museum bought the vase. I couldn't take the job, but it was enormously encouraging when the prospects for designers in England were so bleak.

SILVER SPOON 1952

First-year students at the Royal College of Art's School of Silversmithing were expected to spend some time drawing in the Victoria and Albert Museum, and I made detailed working drawings of a complex Georgian cruet stand.

Only after this were we allowed into the workshop, and this silver spoon was my first job. The festival of Britain had only just closed and the Skylon was an all pervading influence, though in my case, I think, unconsciously.

Sugar spoon.

Bergen vase.

Peppermill, height 115 mm.

Candlestick's, height 140 mm.

HEAL'S SILVER 1967
Skyjalm Petersen said "When you
arrange your exhibition at my shop in
Copenhagen, apart from manufactured
products please also bring your Heal's
silver and some special local food and
drink for the opening party." So I
assembled a collection of silver and
many crates of Garnes home-brewed
Burford ale, and a large Double
Gloucester cheese.

It was only when we reached the
customs at Copenhagen that I realised

that I had forgotten about export documentation; the customs officer asked what we had on three overladen trolleys and I said, going very red, "Oh, just silver, beer and cheese." He stared in disbelief. "Please come this way." Luckily I caught a glimpse of Skjalm just then, waiting to greet me on the far side of the barrier, and he came to our rescue.

Many Danish architects and designers sampled the delights of the double strength Burford beer and, no doubt with its help, the exhibition was a success.

Coffee pot with rosewood handle and knob, height 215 mm.

Condiment set, height 80 mm.

Butter dish, height 125 mm.

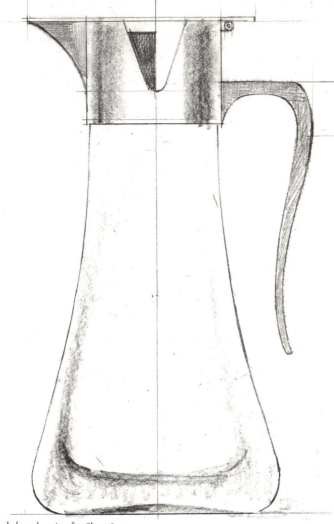

Workshop drawing for Claret Jug.

CLARET JUG & SHIP'S DECANTER 1968
Plain full-lead crystal glassware mounted with polished silver is a very attractive combination as the two materials complement each other in a rather ambiguous way. The problem of tolerance with blown glassware means that it is always necessary to form the silver to fit the glassware and this is especially true with these two examples where the silver mount fits both the outside and inside of the glass.

Claret Jug in lead crystal glass.

Decanter in lead crystal glass.

The Decanter and Claret Jug are made in small batches, approximately six at a time, at infrequent intervals, but even so, it is necessary to make a metal mould for the glass blower to form his glass in. These moulds are expensive and in practice could be used for quantity production. Another factor that creates problems is using uncut lead crystal, which means that any flaws on the glass cannot be hidden and the reject rate of glass can be quite high.

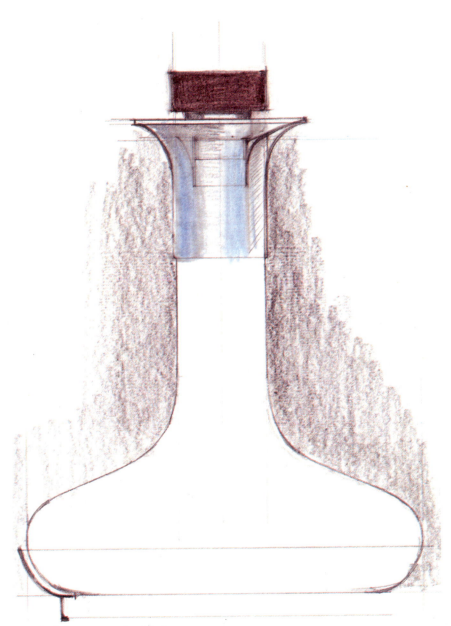

First sketch design in pencil and chalk.

J.B. Tea & Coffee Set 1968

One of my neighbours in the village outside Stratford-upon-Avon where I live was the late J.B. Priestley. He once asked me to design a special pot that would match a fine Georgian Coffee Pot that he owned. I use the word 'match' loosely here – what he wanted was a pot that could be used from day-to-day and that would look like a piece made in the 1970s, but at the same time, it had to harmonise with his own rather ornate Georgian piece.

The first design was for a rounded conical pot with a domed lid, a thumb lift but no knob, and a laminated rosewood handle. Later the shape was changed to something much more curvilinear. Ever since this commission, the series has been known as the 'JB Set'!

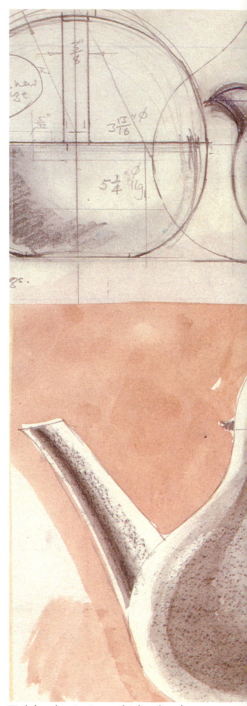

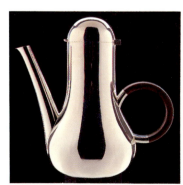

Coffee pot, height 204 mm.

Teapot, height 153 mm.

Workshop drawing in pencil, ink and wash.

30

Teapot with ivory handle and knob, height 105 mm.

DOMESTIC SILVER 1972
There are two great advantages in having a small shop like mine in Chipping Camden which sells your own work. One is that there are no anxieties about the selection of new merchandise. The other is that the shop is like a permanent exhibition where you can meet your customer. New lines for the shop means new design work, so there is always encouragement to add to the collection.

First design sketch, brown ink.

Pencil drawing for sugar bowl.

Coffee pot, height 251 mm.

Design sketch for coffee pot.

Small pitcher with cast handle, height 140 mm.

If you are in touch with customers, you become aware of what seems right, what customers want and the price they are prepared to pay for it. It is the commercial side of art and design, and though it has its drawbacks, it is by and large an excellent thing for a designer to sell his own designs in the market place as well as selling ideas to clients.

There is no doubt that this personal relationship with customers has led to the design of many pieces of domestic silverware that might otherwise never have been produced.

The pieces illustrated on this page all owe their origins to enquiries from customers, and sometimes the piece in question has been named after the client. The coffee service commissioned by Lt. Col. Hackworth is known as 'The Hackworth' and similarly, Col. Morrison's commission for a nice heavy jug to take "just the right amount of water" for his whisky became the 'Morrison' jug.

Tea service with rosewood handle and knob, height 115 mm.

Pencil and wash design sketch.

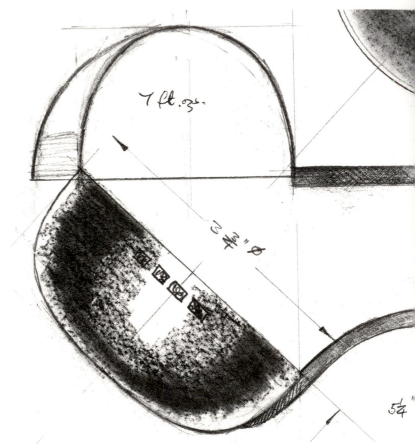

Pencil sketch for punch ladle.

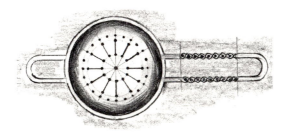

Workshop drawing for tea strainer.

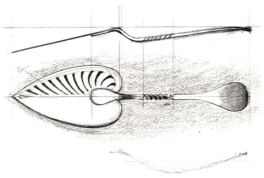

Design sketch for fish server.

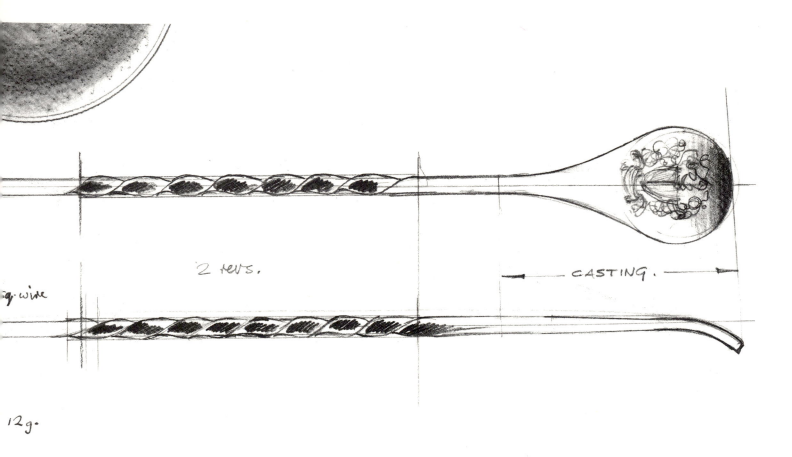

2 revs.

g. wire

CASTING.

12g.

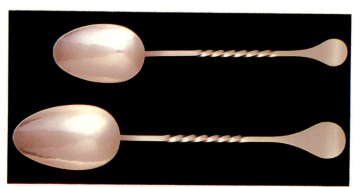

Spoons with twisted handles, length 280 mm and 315 mm.

SILVER SPOONS 1975
This range of silver spoons, ladle, punch
bowl, tea strainer etc., is designed around
the common theme of twisting a square
wire. In many cases the wire is finished
by soldering a cast rounded end which
makes the pieces functional to use.
   The bowls of all the spoons are
hammered, and this provides an
interesting texture with the smooth
finish of the stem and terminal piece.
The first design in this series was a
commissioned ladle (see sketch above).

Preliminary sketch.

BARRIE CANDELABRA 1981
Sometimes the opportunity occurs to
design and make metalwork just to suit
individual pieces of furniture or of an
interior. These candelabra made in brass
are of quite a massive size for one of the
largest and most beautiful refectory
tables that I have ever seen. It is a very
old table and belongs to the Misses Barrie
of Broadway, Worcestershire, who
commissioned the candelabra.

  Sketch designs were proposed but it
turned out to be impossible to judge
whether the table would overpower the
candlesticks or not, and to settle the
matter, a wooden model was made – an
elaborate and costly way of solving the
problem but one that paid dividends in
the end as the candelabra looked quite
handsome in their eventual setting.

Brass candelabra, gilt finish, height 450 mm.

It is often said, and I believe it to be quite true, that specially commissioned work which is aesthetically progressive and interesting, invariably has to be subsidised. Nevertheless, work of this nature has always been the most important aspect of an artist craftsman's repertoire.

As a student at Birmingham College of Art in the early 1950s I received a very thorough training in all aspects of the design of ceremonial plate – hours were spent studying heraldry and lettering and the layout of inscriptions, enamelling, engraving and chasing, and making presentation drawings usually related to ceremonial work. Indeed apart from ecclesiastical work it was generally agreed that the occasional silver commission was as much as anyone dared hope for.

It makes little difference how depressed the state of economy might become, there are always important occasions when a reminder of an event needs to be recorded for posterity, and silver and gold has for centuries fulfilled this requirement – subject of course to the unforeseen hazards of theft and the usual destruction by melting down.

The fact that special commissioned work must be costly in terms of time and effort in design and model-making compared to 'off the shelf' designs, is

Drawing in pencil and wash for fruit bowl, Imperial College, London, 1955.

Watercolour for mazer bowl, 1956.

a point that is not always appreciated, and with the remorseless increase of costs, both of the metal and of the craftsman's time, the possibility of making commissioned work profitable generally declines with the passing of each successive year.

Many silversmiths in England can count themselves fortunate in having such an important and active Livery Company, The Worshipful Company of Goldsmiths, which has for years not only commissioned modern silver for its own fine collection, but has taken a very active role in bringing together the artist craftsman, the donor and recipient for important pieces of ceremonial plate. The activities of the company extend not only to the placing of commissions but also promotion of the craft in every possible way, particularly with exhibitions at home and overseas and publications relating to the craft.

R.I.B.A. badge of office, diameter 50 mm.

The policy of Goldsmiths' Hall has always been to encourage the young craftsman and when I left the Royal College of Art in 1955 I was lucky in being given several commissions through the Company for civic, ecclesiastical and university plate. During the first two years of my workshop, there was a straightforward balance between my work for Old Hall (stainless steel designs) and the commissions I received from recommendations given by Goldsmiths' Hall.

This balance however soon changed as commissioned work tailed off, leaving a serious gap in my workshop activities, and although I have always continued to design and make ceremonial work, it has been on a rather spasmodic basis. The decline in commissioned work in the early '60s did, however, bring some benefits, for it was then that I turned my attention seriously to developing designs in cast iron.

TROPHIES 1960

On certain occasions trophies can be stimulating to design, especially if there is the possibility of incorporating wit and humour in the design.

In 1960 I received an enquiry from the Crafts Centre, then at Hay Hill in Mayfair, 'Would I be interested in designing and making a trophy for the Duke of Edinburgh?'. I was elated, but when I heard that the commission was for a 'Tiddlywinks' trophy, I began to think that it was a practical joke! Not so.

To my surprise, I learned that there was an annual championship match between Oxford and Cambridge Universities, and that the Duke of Edinburgh was the President of the society. After preparing what seemed like hundreds of sketches, I settled on the idea of a spinning wink, mounted on a slender column and set on a rosewood base. On one side of the wink were the Arms of the Duke of Edinburgh, and on the other, the simple designation, 'The Silver Wink'. The wink was counter-weighted so that the arms always came to rest in the correct vertical position.

Another trophy of the same period was not really a design at all, but it solved the problem of the Supreme Award for the Packaging Institute – I chose to make the Award a Golden Egg. In the first instance the egg was packed in a leather cylinder and was weighted so that it rolled into the correct horizontal position and the inscription could be easily read; later it was permanently mounted on a block of marble and so lost its intimate handleable quality.

A few years later in 1962 a trophy was designed for the International Packaging Exhibition, called 'Interplas'; this symbolised the moulding process with a golden ball fitted inside a clear acrylic ball that was split so that the symbolic mould came apart when the top half of

Presentation drawing in pencil and wash for the Gardener's Trophy, 1954.

Football Manager's Trophy.

the acrylic cover was removed. Dieter Rams, who designed for Braun in West Germany, won the award on the three occasions it was given.

My 'black joke' was a trophy for Elastoplast, which ended in a very sharp point; a misdirected flourish of the hand would require an application of the famous product.

A ziggurat was the basis for the 'Football Manager of the Year' trophy, won so many times by Matt Busby and eventually given to him outright. This symbolised the ascent to the top, though not a design that one could hold triumphantly aloft, kiss and run round the football field with. It was given by Westclox as part of a sponsorship programme on which they embarked in the early 1960s. I recall the difficulties I had in persuading the management to proceed with such a design when they had their hearts set on a conventional cup; and these were brave days, and they consented to my proposals.

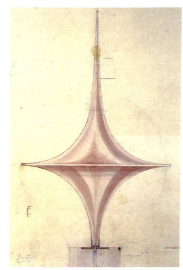

Elastoplast Trophy.

Computer Award for schools.

I look back on these trophies, because they were all produced a long time ago, and it has been many years since I produced a trophy, incorporating the elements that I feel are necessary. The exception is a trophy in bronze for computer programming skills in schools, commissioned by C.P.S. Computers Limited in the late 1970s. It is based on a stylised brain set in juxtaposition to a microchip; the trophy poses the question, 'Who will be master?'

Tiddlywinks' Award, 1960.

The inkstand of 1960 commissioned by
the late Ivan Tarratt for the Civic Plate
collection of Leicester City has always
been one of my favourite designs. I liked
the way in which the mirror-polished
silver, rosewood and optical lens ground
glass were set in juxtaposition, which
seemed to give the stand an almost
architectural quality.

Ironically, I visited an exhibition one
day and saw the inkstand displayed with
the base upside down so that the cubes of
glass projected above the silver box,
thereby completely destroying the
essential element of the design.

For the record, it is illustrated here as
it was designed.

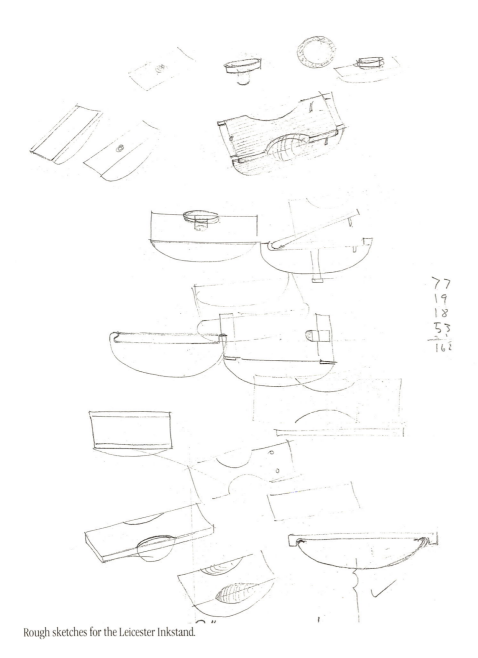

77
19
18
53
___
168

Rough sketches for the Leicester Inkstand.

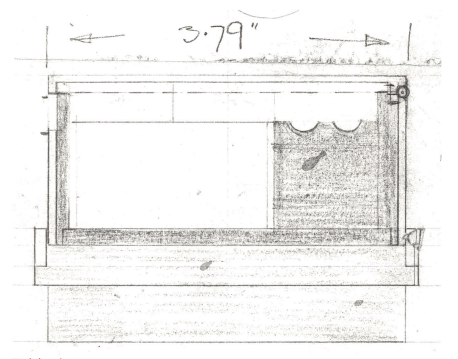

Workshop drawing.

Inkstand with rosewood stand and glass inkwells.

The foundations of Churchill College were being laid when I went to see Sir John Cockcroft to discuss a large silver coffee service he wished to present to the college to commemorate his appointment as the first Master. As well as conventional pots, I proposed a one-gallon coffee urn, for I was sure that if I made ordinary pots to the capacity he had in mind, they would be far too heavy and cumbersome in use.

I found Sir John in a small office surrounded by the drawings of the architect of the college, Richard Sheppard of Sheppard, Robson and Partners. I thought, 'How splendid this is, to discuss a large silver commission for a college that is still a flat building site'. Sir John took no convincing that a coffee urn would be needed.

I also recall the episode of a silver trowel that Richard Sheppard was to present to Sir Winston Churchill at the 'topping off' ceremony. I wondered whether to design a traditional trowel, a beautiful form if ever there was one, or to take artistic licence. Unfortunately, I chose the latter course of development.

Later I was invited to a Fellows' Dinner where Richard Sheppard sought me out. He was a heavily built man who supported himself on a walking stick. He

Coffee urn, cream and sugar bowl.

came close to me and placed his stick firmly on the centre of my shoe, pinning me to the spot; before I could utter a gasp of pain, he gave me a lecture on the beauty of a real trowel and how designers should not take liberties with such splendid objects. The point was fully taken.

The trowel cannot have been held against me, for I received several commissions from the college afterwards, including the large repousse dish which the Bursar, Dr. Armstrong, had specially made to commemorate his term of office.

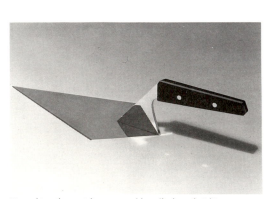

Trowel in silver with rosewood handle, length 340 mm.

Sketch for Churchill College coffee service.

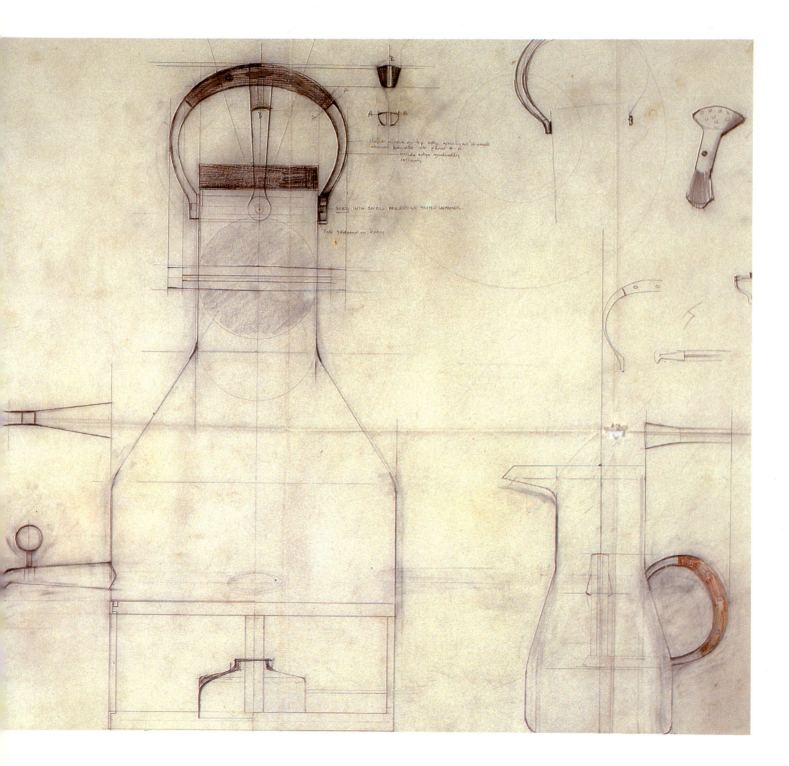

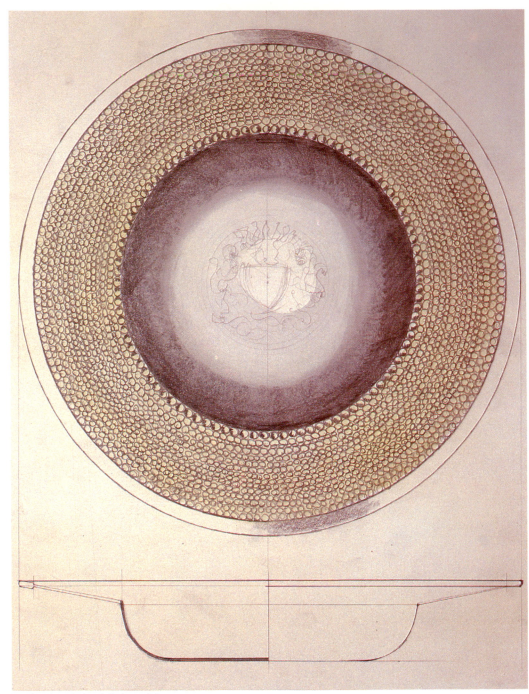

Pencil and wash sketch for large dish.

Dish decorated by repousse work.

Candelabra in silver.

CANDELABRUM 1958

This was the first piece of silver I made for which I did not produce any drawings. Graham Hughes, the Art Director at Goldsmiths' Hall, was assembling a collection of silverware to tour America under the sponsorship of the Smithsonian Institute and he had placed commissions with a number of designers. Gerald Benney made a very original altar set and Louis Osman an extraordinary design for a large platter in which a thick ingot of cast Britannia silver was beaten, by using a ten-pound sledgehammer: the finished plate represented the ultimate statement in wrought silver as all the sledgehammer blows were left on the surface as struck.

I began simply with a model, acquiring lengths of wooden dowelling rods from the local ironmonger and turning these on my lathe in a random series of rounded and waisted forms; and then assembled the candelabrum by a series of random-shaped cross members, glueing the structure together; this was the first occasion that I had presented a design in this way. Graham Hughes of Goldsmiths' Hall then gave me the immediate go-ahead.

Looking back on the design, I felt elated with my pursuit of the accidental effect. It was marvellous to tackle silver in this free, casual way. There was something in the air in those days; I am sure a visit to the Jackson Pollock exhibition at the Whitechapel Art Gallery in 1958, my first encounter with action painting was more than just stimulating.

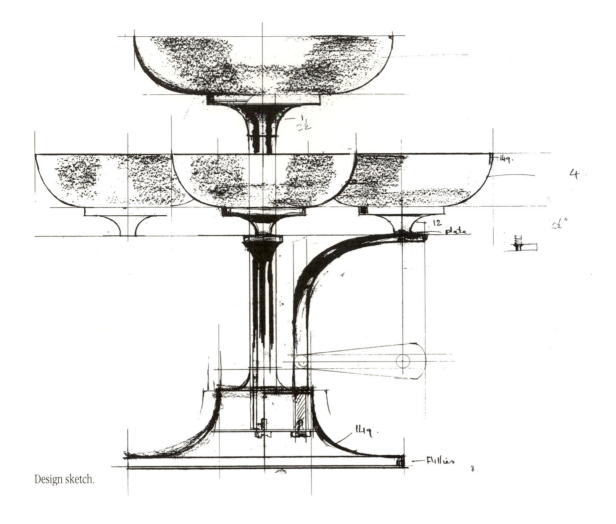

Design sketch.

Silver epergne, height 305 mm.

THE ROYAL SOCIETY OF ARTS 1965
Six candelabra were made in the
Campden workshop during the mid-
'60s together with matching condiment
sets. The candelabra design had its
origins in a commission for Birmingham
University a year or two earlier; on that
occasion five arms were mounted on a
flat base. The modification of the raised
centre to the base and the addition of the
sixth arm greatly improved the design,
and later, in 1982, further small
refinements were incorporated for the
version made for the British Embassy in
Manila.

When the R.S.A. candelabra were
being made Sir William Russell Flint, R.A.,
visited the workshop and was so taken
with the design that he asked if I would
make him a version to present to the
Royal Academy. We corresponded for
some time while he made discreet
enquiries to the House Committee as to
its suitability for R.A. functions, but
unfortunately before the matter was
settled he died. To this day I treasure the
letters he wrote and marvel at his
beautiful calligraphy.

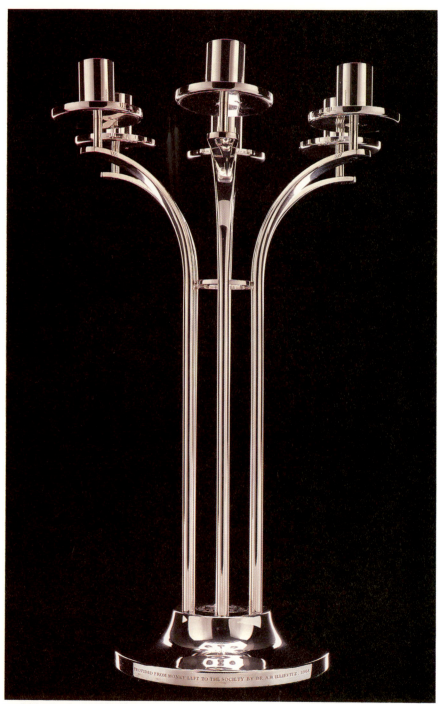

Candelabra in silver, height 460 mm.

GOLDSMITH'S HALL 1968-70

For a long time during 1968 I puzzled over the decoration for two huge silver candelabra commissioned by the Worshipful Company of Goldsmiths; Until quite by chance I got chatting to a man in a remote pub in mid-Wales during a family holday. It turned out that I was talking to Mr. Butler, a Birmingham manufacturer who made the stainless steel condiment set bodies that I had designed for Old Hall, by a process known as rotary swaging.

Determined to leave no stone unturned, I described my candelabra problems, and to my surprise, he said he thought he could help. He had just been to a sale of an old clock and watch factory and had bought a 19th Century machine, more for its antique appearance and rarity value than for its usefulness. It had been used for making ball winders for hunter watches and he was certain he could adapt it to produce the effect I wanted; as he did, perfectly, after many experiments on various tubes.

The tubes were all eventually shaped, and after months of workshop activity, Paul Heneghan and John Limbrey assembled and completed the commission. I then told John Houston, the curator of Goldsmiths' Hall that it was ready for delivery.

The candelabra had to be presented to the Court of the Company during their next meeting, and it was an anxious moment for it had been impossible to convey in sketches or models the appearance of the finished design. During the afternoon of the presentation I waited for the news, and eventually John Houston telephoned to say it had been an unqualified success.

There was, however, some bad news. One of the candelabra had fallen off a trolley on its way to the vaults and one side was completely crushed on the stone floor, 'Would we repair it as soon as possible?'. I went into the workshop, gave the good news and then the bad, and retreated to my studio. The brand new candelabra was duly rebuilt.

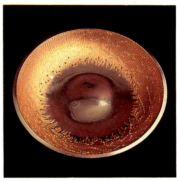

Silver dish parcel gilt, diameter 500 mm.

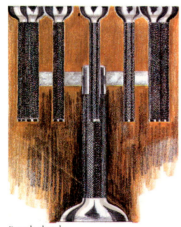

Rough sketch.

Candelabra in silver parcel gilt.

AMETHYST DISH 1973

The making of this dish was a TOUR DE FORCE of fine craftsmanship by John Limbrey as each of the tiny settings for the amethysts and the swirling rhythmic wirework had to be soldered onto the surface of a very large bowl. The problems of avoiding an accidental melt of a wire or setting can well be imagined.

The dish was made for the CRAFTSMAN'S ART exhibition held at the Victoria and Albert Museum in 1973, and is now in a private collection.

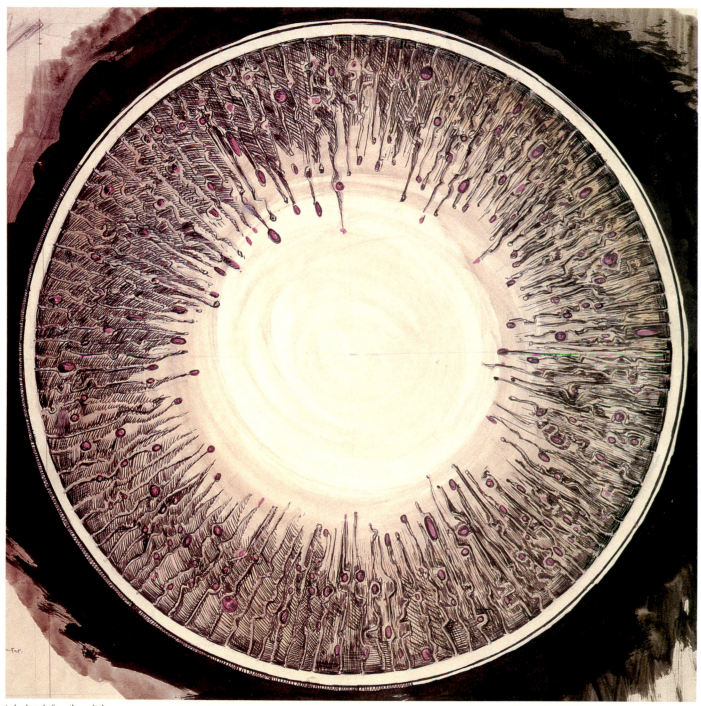

Ink sketch for silver dish.

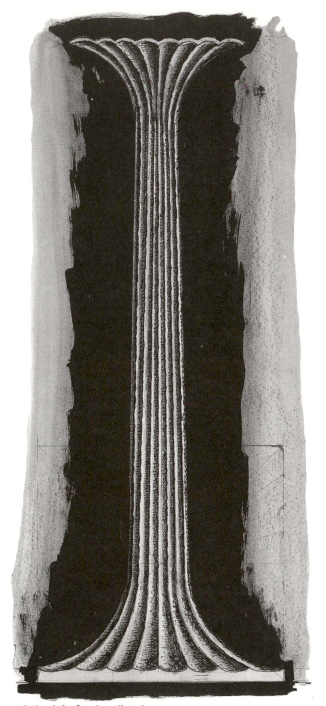

Ink sketch for fluted candlestick.

Workshop sketch for candlestick base.

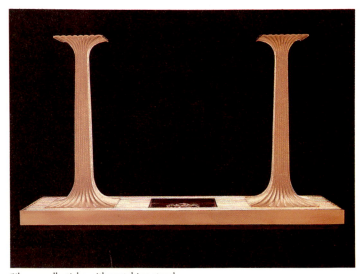

Silver candlesticks with matching stand.

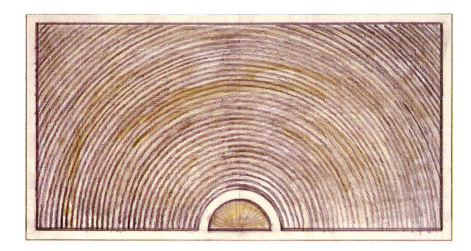

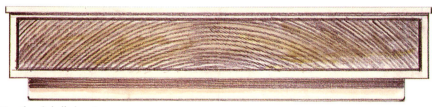

Pencil and chalk drawing.

I have always preferred silver which is mainly unadorned, but some occasions seem to call for a different approach; a box, for instance, which does not show finger marks saves on cleaning. In the two examples illustrated, the texture has been achieved by hammering or punching the silver over a specially treated cast iron former, so that the surface shows pronounced tooling marks on one side and the same hammer marks, but with a granular texture on the other.

I first used this technique on the Courvoisier cigar box and the difference between the outer and inner surface can be seen when the lid is opened. The same principle applies to the candlesticks presented by G.K.N. to the City of Birmingham: outer and inner surfaces are visible round the candle-socket. A texture as strong as this is not always appropriate, and these are the only occasions when I have experimented with this technique using cast iron.

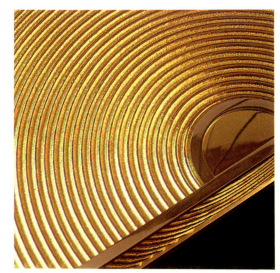

Silver gilt cigar box.

Design sketch for the Tower of London goblet.

BASE PLAN.

RW. 5.77.

TOWER OF LONDON GOBLET 1978

I have never liked limited edition marketing and, during the 1970s, scarcely a colour supplement appeared which did not offer a commemorative article, often made in silver, and in edition numbers so large that the rarity value was non-existent. Few of these commemorative pieces were worthwhile, and nearly always the products were manufactured, although the term, 'hand crafted' was used to describe essentially mechanical processes.

The market reached its peak at the time of The Queen's Silver Jubilee in 1977 and declined with the beginning of the recession and, in the case of silver, commodity speculators driving the price of the metal to an unprecedented level.

The commission to make a goblet to commemorate the 900th anniversary of The Tower of London was one that I therefore approached with misgivings, but the brief given by The Department of the Environment for an edition of only 50 goblets, each to embody making techniques that were entirely reliant on handwork, eventually aroused my enthusiasm. So designs were prepared.

The base was made of five lobes, like a medieval chalice, and the lettering was cut in Gothic script on a hatched background; the bowls were all hand raised. It was just as well that 1978 was not a busy year in the Campden workshop, for John Limbrey worked long and hard to complete the goblets in time for the celebrations.

As things turned out the selling of the goblets was quite different from that of the usual commercial limited editions; and at the price of £790.00 each in 1978, this must have been one of the most exclusive editions ever offered. In all the celebrations and publicity for the event and souvenir articles that had been specially produced, there was not even a mention of the goblet, and to tell the truth I was relieved. I learnt later that all of them had been sold, presumably through very discreet advertising or by word of mouth.

Goblet in silver parcel gilt, height 190 mm.

Crayon drawing for wine flagon.

Pair of silver wine flagons, height 266 mm.

Pair of silver loving cups.

LOVING CUPS 1977
The Worshipful Company of Furniture-makers became a very important patron in the late 1970s, largely thanks to Geoffrey Dunn, famous for his patronage of design and his splendid shop in Bromley, Kent. His infectious enthusiasm and advice proved invaluable as he guided the progress of such pieces as the pair of large loving cups presented by the Livery Company to mark the Silver Jubilee of Her Majesty Queen Elizabeth II.

I had developed a rather elegant design, but Geoffrey said, "Make good solid drinking pots with knobbed covers that you can bang like a saucepan lid – remember these cups are used after Livery Dinners!" This excellent advice was incorporated in the finished pieces.

Pencil sketch.

Wooden model of coffee urn body.

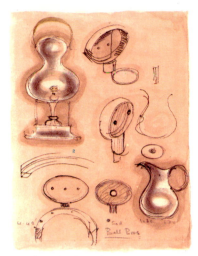

Page from sketch book.

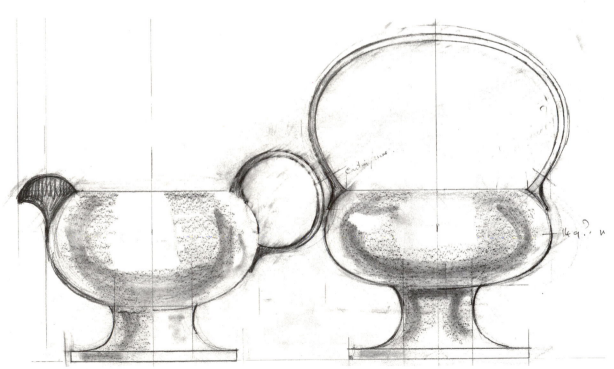

Workshop drawing for cream and sugar bowl.

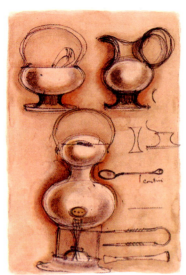
Page from sketch book.

COFFEE SERVICE, ST. LUCIA 1979
This complete coffee service represents a second statement on this particular theme, the first being the coffee urn of 1960 commissioned by Sir John Cockcroft for Churchill College, Cambridge. Twenty-two years later the forms are rounded and hammered, but the essential components remain the same: the swing handle on the urn with secret stop device, both front and rear, inlaid with rosewood, the heater, tap and stand. The urn is engraved with the full Coat of Arms of St. Lucia and 24 coffee spoons completed the service.

The coffee service was commissioned by P.S.A. Suppliers on behalf of The Foreign and Commonwealth Office, as the British Government's gift to St. Lucia to commemorate indepedence, 1979.

Urn, height 330 mm.

Pencil and wash workshop drawing.

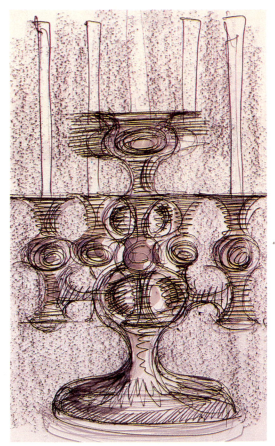

Preliminary design sketch.

VICTORIA & ALBERT 1980
It proved to be a very sobering thing, once the first pleasure of the commission had subsided, to be asked to design a piece of silver for the collection of the Victoria and Albert Museum, for I knew that I was embarking on a piece that, all being well, would remain in the collection in perpetuity.

The brief merely stated that I should design a pair of silver candelabra; making a start on a job like that is definitely not easy. I resorted to my life-

Pair of silver candelabra, height 335 mm.

long technique of problem solving by walking on the Malvern Hills. I grew up on the west side of these hills and throughout my life every major problem has been solved in this way. Even after many hours of walking I find that I have not really looked or noticed anything on the way, rather in a trance.

Gradually the theme emerged, a candelabram of round juicy shapes echoing the St. Lucia coffee service commission, but nevertheless I was apprehensive of the danger of producing a feeling of ungainly solidity and massiveness.

I decided to approach the problem in a very relaxed way, just some tentative sketches leaving plenty of room for refining and altering at a later date. I showed a few of these sketches to Shirley Bury, then Deputy Keeper of Metalwork, Claude Blair, the Keeper, and Sir Roy Strong; and to my joy they all agreed on the sketch that I myself liked most.

The design was made as a wooden model for size and final approval, then the two silver candelabra were made by John Limbrey in my workshop.

When I delivered the pieces, Sir Roy Strong said, "This is the first silver the Victoria and Albert has commissioned since the days of Sir Henry Cole." To mark the occasion he had the candelabra engraved with the following inscription – "TENABRAS FUGO: OCULOS LAETOR: NOCTEM CORONANS. R.S. ME FIERI FECIT: V & A 1980." (I put darkness in flight, rejoice the eyes, crowning the night. R.S. caused me to be made. V & A 1980.)

64

Sketch for dish.

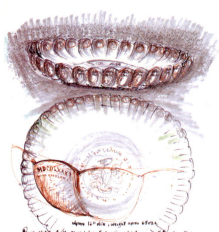

Original design for client.

Engraving detail.

This dish was commissioned by Lucian Ercolani, Master of the Worshipful Company of Furnituremakers, in 1981. It seemed appropriate in the year of the Royal Wedding that it should be made in Britannia silver, with a special Hall Mark.

The hallmark is struck within a circular band of lettering surrounding the Coat of Arms. The Arms and the dates engraved on the flutes are orientated in relation to the hallmark.

The dish has 47 deep concave flutes, each flute representing a term of office for each of the Masters of the Worshipful Company of Furnituremakers during the 20th century. The tip of the flute containing the engraving for the year 2000 is parcel gilt.

Fluted dish in Britannia silver, diameter 405 mm.

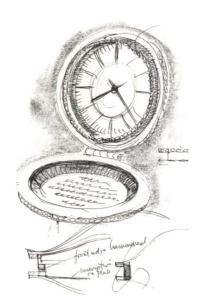

Sketch book drawings for a silver clock.

SURPRISE CLOCK 1983

In 1983 the Birmingham Assay Office wished to make a gift to the Worshipful Company of Goldsmiths, to commemorate an important event, but the question was, what could be given that the Goldsmiths' Company did not already possess. Being one of the oldest and wealthiest City Livery Companies, their unique collection of plate contained every object imaginable. Hence the idea of a clock that did not look like a clock and that could be used by the Prime Warden during banquets to keep an eye on the timing of events and speakers.

The clock was presented to the Goldsmiths' Company in 1984. Kenneth Grimsley chose a poem by Swift to be engraved inside the clock.

Clock, parcel gilt, in the open position, height 350 mm.

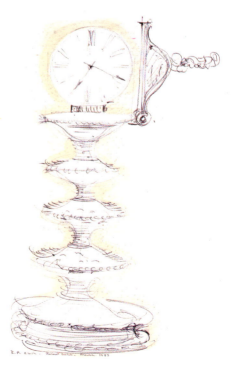

Ball point pen and wash drawing.

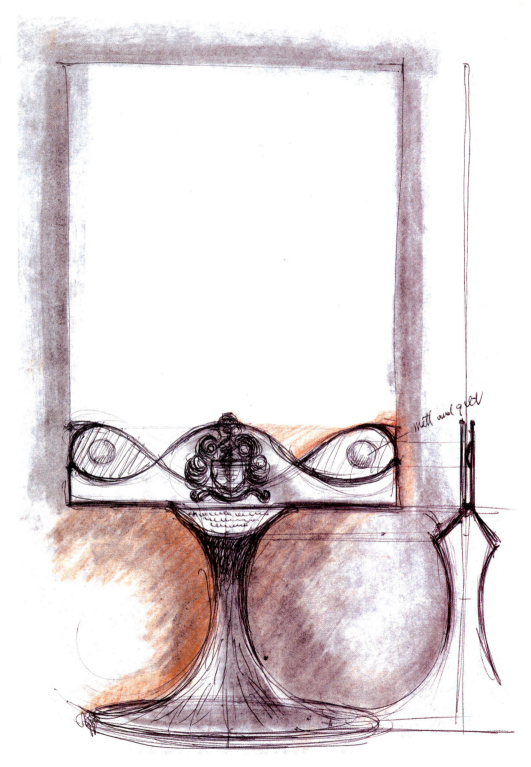

matt and gilt

68

PLACE SETTING HOLDER 1984
There are often ancient institutions
which like the Worshipful Company of
Goldsmiths have acquired fine collections
of silver over the years; they pose the
same difficulties in choosing a suitable
gift. In the Company of Cutlers in
Hallamshire it is the custom each year for
the Master Cutler to commemorate his
term of office with a gift to the company.

In 1984 the retiring Master had no
doubt about what he wished to present.
Guests of the Company needed to know
in advance where they were sitting when
they dined at the Hall so a table and
seating plan holder was the apt choice,

a novel idea as a piece of presentation silver, not unrelated to the small menu holders that used to regularly grace the elegant table settings of yesterday.

The design was created with the idea of giving a prominent display to the full coat of arms of the Company, engraved in the near vertical position. A removable and if necessary replaceable sheet of polished clear acrylic supports the information.

The engraving on this piece was undertaken by George Lukes who since 1975 has been responsible for most of the engraving on the ceremonial silverware illustrated in this book.

Table seating holder in silver and acrylic, height 350 mm.

Sketch book drawing of Embassy table, ink and wash.

The British Embassy, Manila 1982

The tableware represents the accumulation of a large number of designs spanning nearly 30 years work.

The cutlery used was the Alveston pattern of 1962, condiment sets, peppermills and butter dishes etc. were from the Heal's range of 1965, the candelabra were very similar to the R.S.A. commission of 1965 and the serving ware was made from the ORIANA commission of 1958.

The new addition was a silver centrepiece in the form of a rosebowl and all these pieces were completed and delivered just in time to the P.S.A. for the opening of the Embassy in 1983 with sufficient tableware for 24 people to dine.

It was interesting to see that the completed table had a unified appearance despite the great gaps between the creation of the various designs.

Sketch book drawing.

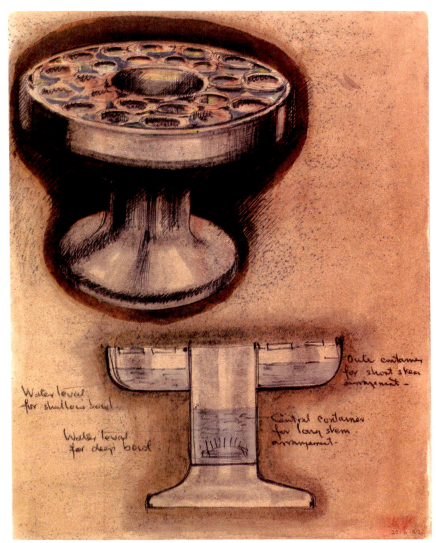

Water level
for shallow bowl

Water level
for deep bowl

Outer container
for short stem
arrangement -

Central container
for long stem
arrangement -

Sketch book drawing for rose bowl.

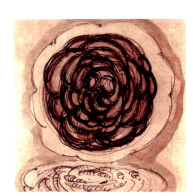

Sketch book drawing.

Rose bowl silver parcel gilt.

THE MANILA CENTREPIECE

The design began with some rough sketches of roses which soon led to the development of a formal pierced grid and the shape had to closely relate to the remainder of the tableware.

The centrepiece is really two separate bowls, each capable of holding separate supplies of water, made as one single unit.

The central container is to hold tall stemmed flowers and the outer is shallow for flower heads and buds.

When arranged, a pronounced conical effect is created, and without flowers, it makes a decorative centrepiece.

Selection of tableware in silver and silver plate.

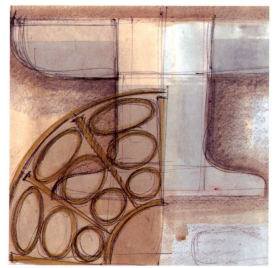

Sketch book drawing.

RIYADH 1984

I was approached by The Crown Suppliers on behalf of the Foreign and Commonwealth Office to investigate the possibility of designing tableware for the new Ambassador's residence in Riyadh and, as is the norm these days, Government departments have to operate on a very tight budget.

The Foreign and Commonwealth Office wanted an outline proposal to see how far they could stretch their budget. As I have never really liked silverplate,

and as sterling silver was too expensive, I suggested pewter. The enquiry was by telephone from John Pound, Design Manager of The Crown Suppliers, and when I mentioned pewter there was a long silence. I thought we had been cut off and anxiously enquired if he was still on the line. "Did I hear correctly? Pewter, for the Ambassador's table?"

Visions of dark oxidised pewter shapes had no doubt stunned him into silence. I was determined to press home the option and we arranged a meeting at

the Design Centre the following day; I took along samples of hand-beaten pewter with a highly polished finish. The edges were heavily thickened by beating the pewter back on itself, so that they shimmered with a pleasing reflection.

The first hurdle was over. "It looks rather nice," said John. "I will show it to some of my colleagues and let you know if you should go any further. "On the basis of the small articles shown it was agreed that at least the committee should be given the opportunity of examining

Sketch book study for pewter.

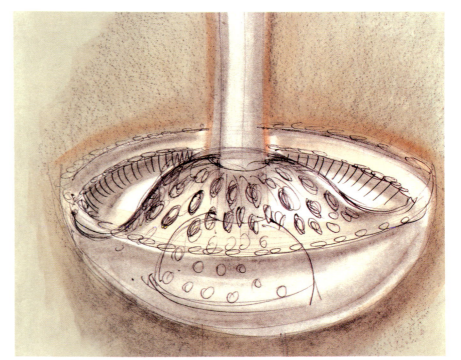

Drawing in ink and sepia wash for centre-piece.

some specially designed pieces – so the concept of a new collection began. I felt that a re-assessment of the metal was long overdue, and was glad of the opportunity to try it out.

As the main table was capable of being broken down into four small units, the traditional single centrepiece was replaced by tall, robust condlesticks, so made that each of them could be combined with a small removable rose bowl. The design was presented as a wooden model, and then, within a

Sketch book study, not used.

matter of two weeks I had to have the finished article in pewter ready for the committee to see: quite a problem as we had never really worked in pewter before. We engaged the help of a professional pewtersmith, Bernard Butler, who worked with John Limbrey, and on the appointed day the centrepiece was ready. I could scarcely believe it when I received a telephone call from John Pound to say that the committee was delighted, and that we were to go ahead with a complete table-setting.

Centrepiece in the form of candleholder and rose bowl, height 370 mm.

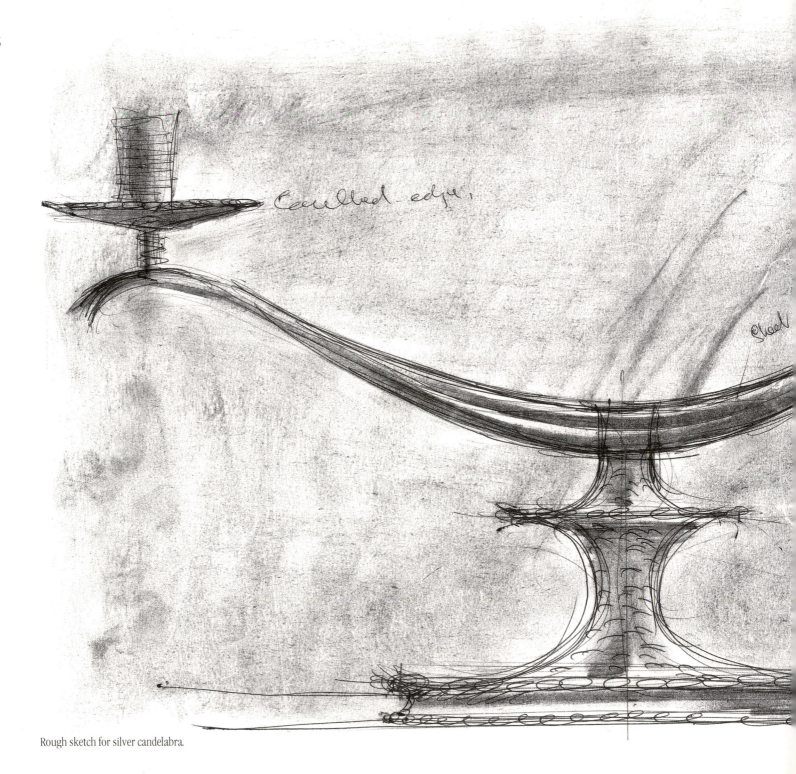

Cerulled edge.

Rough sketch for silver candelabra.

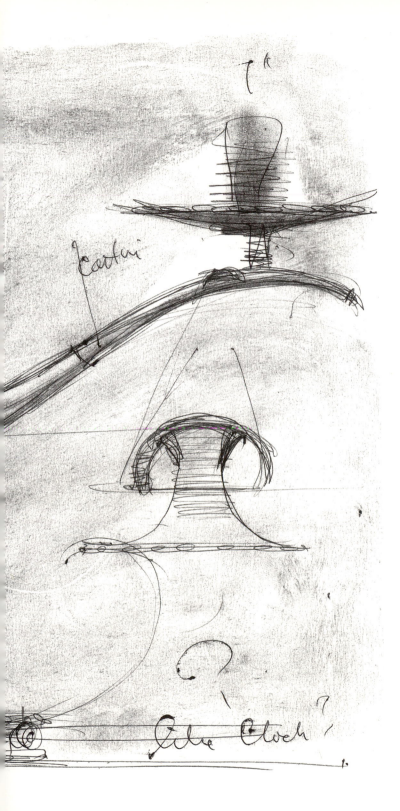

THE BRITISH MUSEUM 1983

Of all the candelabra designs that I have produced the brief given to me by Sir David Wilson, Director of the British Museum, was the most precise and exact I have ever received.

"It should be low and graceful, like a Viking Boat, and hold only two candles."

I prepared my designs on the return train as I visualised exactly what he wanted. The next day John began work on a model and when I made the next appointment to see Sir David Wilson, I said, "I hope you like this as I have nothing else to show on this occassion."

All was well – I heaved a sigh of relief as the design was approved, and six candelabra were duly made in my workshop by John Limbrey; the arms were hammered from sheet silver.

They were presented to the British Museum in memory of Pamela Hartwell, by a group of her friends and each candelabra was engraved with a dedication and the donor's name.

Pair of silver candelabra from a set of six, length 420 mm.

ECCLESIASTICAL SILVER

My early training in silversmithing had done much to prepare me for the design problems encountered with a wide variety of religious vessels – careful studies of the history of the chalice and ciborium as well as the functional aspects of administering the holy sacrament were very well researched. However, I must confess that I was not prepared for my first professional assignment in ecclesiastical silver, which was to design and make a pair of reliquaries to hold two sacred relics, for the Church of St. Thomas of Canterbury in the Fulham Road, London. One was a piece of the true cross and the other a fragment of the bone of St. Thomas A Becket. The workshop was barely operational in late autumn 1955 when I prepared sketches and eventually took possession of the sacred relics. I was overawed at the thought of what the two capsules contained and at the time, not being in possession of a safe, I made a secure hiding place for them on top of an old beam that spanned the workshop, close to my sleeping quarters. The job progressed slowly and painstakingly, and I distinctly recall my vow not to use even the mildest oath when things went wrong lest retribution should fall on my head! Happily the reliquaries were finished in good time and were delivered early in 1956. The early days of the workshop were a busy period for ecclesiastical commissions. After the completion of the ciborium I was at work on a silver alms dish for St. Luke's Church, Holmes Chapel, given in memory of John and Mary Ramsden, a silver and gold pectoral cross, signet and episcopal ring for the Bishop of Bangor and a wafer box for Aldermaston Church.

Ecclesiastical commissions have been an important part of the silversmith's art since time immemorial, and there are many attractions to this kind of work – the wide range of objects that may be commissioned, and the opportunity for relating the pieces to their eventual destination by the use of emblems, the association of Saints, and architectural motifs, and many other associations.

At the same time, I have always found great satisfaction in designing for churches because, apart from the symbolism, there is often a very real functional problem to be solved, e.g. a chalice must work well by being correctly balanced, strongly constructed, and precisely shaped to answer its purpose. It is also encouraging to feel that these vessels will be regularly used and lovingly cared for.

In recent years, however, the high cost of silver and the increase in labour cost, coupled with the

Reliquary, watercolour and indian ink.

Holmes Chapel Alms dish, 1955.

widespread increase in theft, has changed the situation dramatically. The security of crosses and candlesticks is uppermost in the minds of the authorities and the method of safely securing the pieces to the altar or to the wall have an important bearing on the design; even with those safeguards insurance premiums are high. The result has been a move to metals such as brass, bronze, iron or stainless steel, each of which can offer the most interesting solution to the problem, but does little to further the art of the silversmith.

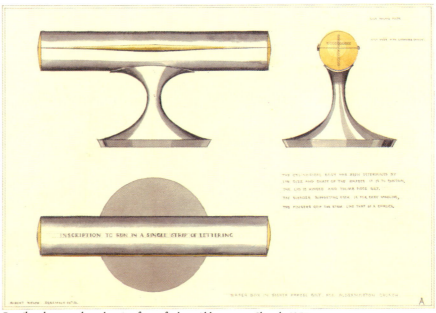

Pencil and watercolour drawing for wafer box, Aldermaston Church, 1957.

Water ewer and lavabo bowl.

Chalice and ciborium.

ST. MARY'S, SWANSEA 1958 – 65

In 1984 I designed and made some church silver for St. Margaret's church at Penn in Buckinghamshire. It was a memorial to my first important patron for ecclesiastical silver, Cyril Davies, and it reminds me of this earlier work.

It was in 1958 that we first met, through an introduction arranged by the Worshipful Company of Goldsmiths. He wished to commission a memorial to his mother and father in the form of a High Altar Cross and candlesticks, to present to St. Mary's, Swansea, a church that had been so badly damaged by bombing in the war that it had to be completely rebuilt and re-dedicated in 1958.

It was the beginning of a long association, not only with Mr. Davies, but also with Canon Davies, who continued to place commissions for the church up to the mid 'sixties. The cross and candlesticks of 1958 remained the dominant theme for all subsequent design commissions which included a wide variety of vessels.

Altar candlesticks.

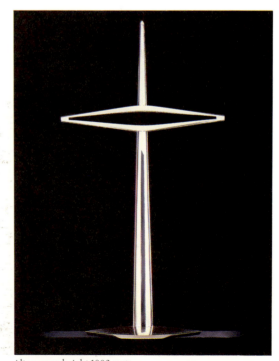

Altar cross, height 1003 mm.

Altar bowl with pierced cover.

FLOWER BOWL 1966
The Chapel of Gordonstoun School was designed by the architect, Patrick Higgins, an old boy of the school.

It is a very simple building and this large circular silver flower bowl is the only ornament on the altar table. The cover is formed from an undulating circular plate which has concentric piercings to take floral arrangements, and the bowl is decorated by the pupils of the school. It was presented by the Midland Group of Friends of Gordonstoun.

CHURCH SILVER AND LOCAL MOTIFS
In the introduction to this section I mentioned that on occasions the opportunity arose for relating ecclesiastical silver to a specific aspect of a church or its neighbourhood.

The Madonna Lily, is the beautiful emblem of the Church at Elmley Castle in Worcestershire, 'The Lily' was applied to a wafer box by a technique known as cut card work. The design was first saw pierced from a sheet of silver then carved and engraved before it was finally pinned on to the lid of the box.

Wafer box with applied madonna lily, 78 mm x 132 mm.

Madonna Lily, in pencil, ink, charcoal and wash, collection, The Reverend George Burgess.

Wall mounted cross in silver and rosewood with repousse pebble decoration, height 1008 mm.

Detail of chalice knop.

Malched pan

Sketch book study for chalice and wafer box.

This work was executed by the late Theodore Wise, one of the most eminent engravers of his day. He was also responsible for carving the knob of the chalice made for Nelson Cathedral, New Zealand, where the selected motif was the white fern of New Zealand.

The Bridport Cross was based on the motif of the nearby Chesil Beach which extends for many miles and the pebbles are naturally graded in size from large to small along its length, to the degree that it is said that a local fisherman could accurately tell his position on the beach in the dead of night just by feeling the size of the pebbles.

Detail.

Pencil and watercolour drawing of pectoral cross for the Bishop of Pontefract.

Brass candlestick with lead crystal shade.

Brass candlestick, height 578 mm.

BRASS CANDLESTICKS, CYPRUS 1974
Revolutions and invasions do not often impinge on design, but there was one occasion when I was glad that I had my car radio tuned to the news. I was on my way to Heathrow to send an air freight parcel containing a pair of large brass altar candlesticks to Cyprus to complete a special commission for St Andrew's Church, Kyrenia. The newscaster announced a Turkish invasion of Cyprus and fighting round Kyrenia. Discretion being the better part of valour, I turned the car round and headed back home, where the package was stored away.

It was to be nearly two years before the candlesticks were safely received at St Andrew's Church. The design was later modified and occassionally made for sale in the Studio Shop.

92

Sketch book study.

TWO CHALICES 1975
By an unusual coincidence two local
churches commisssioned chalices in 1975
– one was for St. Leonard's Church, Clent
and the other for St. Chad's Church,
Bishop Tachbrook, Warwickshire.

The Clent chalice incorporated the
motif of the chains of St. Leonard in the
knop, by using a section of silver chain
soldered into a recess in the knop.

The St. Chad's chalice was designed
with a column to take the engraved
symbol of the medical profession.

plan of knop

Sketch book studies.

hollow flutes.

full flutes.
to match shape of
base and round
bowl.

Sketch book study.

Chalice in silver parcel gilt.

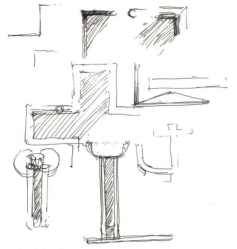

Sketch book notes.

CANTERBURY CATHEDRAL 1979
The technique developed for this commission owes its origin to the shimmering effect of the Goldsmiths' Hall candelabra, but on this occasion the effect was achieved in an entirely different way. Half-round sections of silver wire were indented with a pattern of hollows in a controlled way to achieve the effect of a random pattern. The wires were then assembled side by side and when the most satisfactory juxtaposiion of pattern had been achieved the wires were soldered and then cut into the required shapes. In the case of the Cross the assembled wires were inlaid into a rosewood surround and mounted on a rosewood base. A full sized model of the cross and a candlestick were made and approved before work in silver began.

The commission came from the Chairman of Council and Members of the St. John Ambulance Brigade in Kent, hence the St. John's crosses set in a block of clear acrylic on the base of the candlesticks and the Altar Cross.

Silver cross mounted on rosewood, height 1008 mm. Candlesticks made in silver plate.

Sketch for set of communion plate.

Rough sketch for chalice.

In the early 1980s all the communion silver of St. Peter and St. Paul, Bromley in Kent, was stolen and the insurance values were out of date because American speculators had been inflating the price of silver. Fortunately the church had kept very precise dimensioned records of all the stolen pieces, and through Geoffrey Dunn I was asked to make the communion plate anew, but in silverplate. I took my cue from some stolen Elizabethan chalices and so there is no traditional knop, but a series of half-round rings, which relates all the replacement articles to each other.

Communion plate, silver plated and parcel gilt.

Sketch book study.

I know it is very a fanciful thought, but my present Indian design work produced in Chipping Campden and sent out to Kerala, South India, does have echoes of a previous association that existed before in Chipping Campden at the turn of this century. From 1907 to 1910, Ananda Coomaraswamy, who was to become one of the most distinguished historians of Indian Art, lived in Broad Campden, drawn here, it seems, by the presence of C. R. Ashbee and the Guild of Handicraft, who had moved to the Mill in 1902.

On my first day in my workshop in 1953, as I was helping to remove various articles stored in the old cabinetmakers' workshop of the Guild, I came across Coomaraswamy's Vena, a superb stringed musical instrument which I later acquired. There were also hundreds of Coomaraswamy's photographic glass negatives to be rescued from oblivion during the clearing out, all of which I stored away carefully. I felt instinctively that these were important archive material, although at the time my first concern was to get my workshop operational, and I have to confess that I had very little knowledge of Ashbee's Guild, and even less of Coomaraswamy's amazing role in documenting Indian art, first in Campden then later in India and finally in America where he became Keeper of the Asiatic Department at the Boston Museum.

I wonder if he would have approved of the Campden-India connection of the 1980s?

My first visit to India in a professional capacity was in 1975 when by invitation of the All India Handicraft Board, I undertook a general survey of Indian art metalwork, travelling extensively during a ten-week tour, visiting many remote workshops.

Among the suggestions and recommendations that I made I drew particular attention to the bronze casting of Kerala, and eventually I began a design programme working closely with a number of Government bodies associated with the crafts, namely the All India Handicraft Board, Handloom and Handicraft Export Corporation of Delhi, and the National Institute of Design in Ahmedabad.

My brief has been to help to try and establish export markets for the superlative skills of a particular craft practised in Kerala, South India, bronze casting by the lost-wax method, a craft as old as man himself. The work that is produced is truly amazing – they make huge bowls of thin wall section and of beautiful proportions, sometimes six feet in diameter, and the tall, robust oil lamps used in temples and to illuminate the performance of the famous Kata Kali dancers.

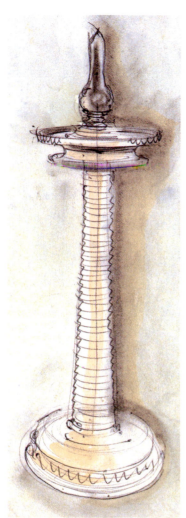

Lamp, Trivandrum Museum.

Not surprisingly, these workshops need many more orders if they are to survive, as bowls for temple feasts and lamps for dancers are not, in modern marketing terms, growth areas.

I love India as a country to visit and to research my subject, to gather information, to meet old friends and to make new ones, to travel to remote workshops, make sketches and drawings, but I am quite unable to create in the field suitable designs that seem right for their purpose.

India can be so overwhelming, the riot of colour and pattern, the smells, the heat, the number of human beings, the hundreds of thousands of clever craftsmen, the seemingly limitless possibilities for design, the sheer frustration of poor communications and travel, the difficulties of obtaining raw materials and the immense size of the country are just a few of the reasons why I have resisted as strongly as possible the temptation to commence design work there and then while in the country. Instead I reserve my thoughts for the cool and temperate well ordered calm of my studio in Chipping Campden and send out the work in the form of carefully finished models with templates, drawings and precise instructions and wait anxiously to see the finished result. Indian metal work can be the least pleasing branch of all the handicrafts practised in India today. Brass and Copper are particularly difficult metals to deal with, especially when they are treated with an abundance of decoration and often rather poorly finished, and in the more sophisticated markets of the West they have little appeal, much less for instance than textiles and carpets from India.

With this range of bronze ware from Kerala I have attempted to distil the flavour of the traditional form of this craft and by concentrating on shape and precise mouldings, the workshops are able to finish the bronze ware to a very high standard, far removed from the ethnic look. Thus the possibility arises for blending together the skills of craftsmen (who incidentally number several thousand) and offering an input to their craft, which is basically product design linked with marketing directions.

It is with the last element, related not just to shape and form alone, but to products suitable for the western market place that it may be possible to complete the equation.

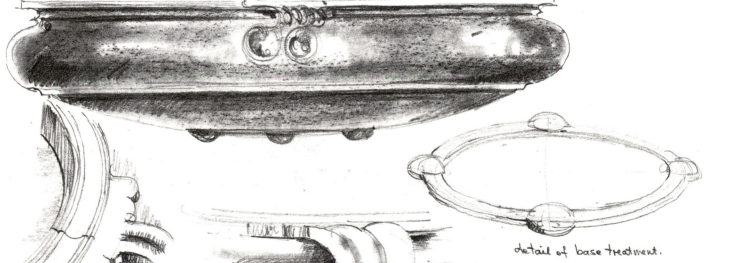

5 ft diameter.

detail of base treatment.

Kerala. Sketch of a beautiful varpu bowl, a superb example of the bell metal workers craft. Trichur museum Nov. 30th

Sketch book drawing of varpu bowl, Trichur Museum.

THE MAKING PROCESS

The process starts with the gathering of clay dried in the sun for several hours. The clean clay is used with water and kept for 24 hours. The clay is then mixed with rice husks to the ratio of five to one, kneaded into clay balls and from these the cone is made.

The castings are constructed around the cone, which is a cylinder with a hole through the centre which forms the axle. It is later fitted to the hand operated lathe and from the cone the desired shape of the vessel is built up in clay, each layer being allowed to dry in the sun. When the basic form is made it is then coated with a fine paste of burnt clay and dried. This burnt clay is taken from moulds previously used and discarded.

Throughout all the processes that follow it should be noted that husks have a very important function. When the time arrives for castings, they enable the hot gases to escape evenly all over the mould, consequently castings of a very high quality are produced.

Craftsman applying wax.

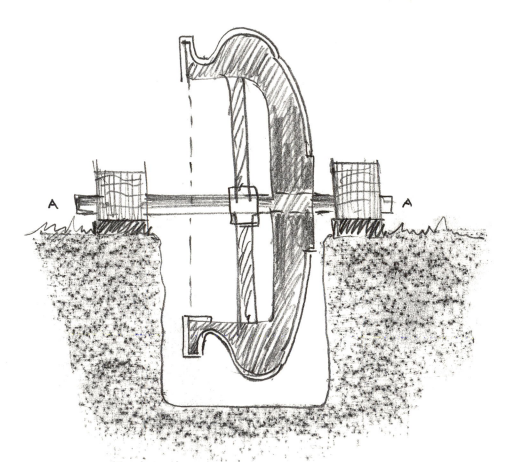

Section of bowl ready for turning.

PREPARATION OF WAX

Fine beeswax is used with aromatic resin in the proportion of one to three, and with every pound of wax, six ounces of castor oil is added, then heated in an earthen pot and finally filtered through a fine cotton cloth into a pot containing cold water. Ten minutes later the wax is removed, kneaded by hand, then rolled and cut into discs one inch thick and five inches in diameter; these are then stored in vessles containing hot water.

The mould is now fitted on to a rudimentary lathe in the form of a simple mechanism comprising a small wooden wheel and a rod passing through it. Two wooden stands that act as bearings are then fitted on either side.

The wax is now applied to the mould to the metal thickness required. The lathe is gently turned by hand and with a heated tool the wax is evenly spread on the mould until the desired shape is turned, then the decoration is modelled. One cannot imagine such beautiful work being made with such simple tools – this is the real art of Bronze Casting in Kerala.

Craftsman turning varpu bowl.

COVERING THE WAX
The paste of burnt clay applied evenly over the wax (several times). When dried there is a thick outer coating. A final coating of clay mixed with rice husk is applied together with broken pieces of tiles and stuck on the outer covering to be sure that the mould is held firmly.

An opening is provided for evacuating the wax and also for pouring in the molten metal and the outer coating is allowed to dry out thoroughly in the sun for approximately one day.

Preparing bowl for casting.

Coconut shell oven, prepared ready for casting.

MELTING OUT THE WAX
The mould is placed in a pit, covered with dry coconut shells and fired, the wax is melted out and runs into a small pit where it is collected and purified.

The casting process.

The metal is melted in crucibles made of clay, charcoal and rice husks. Goatskin bellows are blown until the metal is liquid, the heated mould is buried in earth, leaving only the pouring aperture visible. It takes about 6-8 hours to melt the metal and when cast the mould remains buried in earth until it cools down. When sufficiently cool the outer covering is carefully broken and the cone removed. The projecting metal rod (the pouring channel) is removed by filing, but at this stage it is very brittle.

Prepared moulds drying in the sun.

ANNEALING

The vessel has to be heated until it is dull red and swiftly immersed in hot water, allowing it to cool down before removal.

Costly articles that have very thin wall thickness are tempered in sesame oil, but great care has to be taken to ensure that the oil does not ignite.

Section through a mould.

108

Wax being melted out over a fire.

FINAL PROCESS: POLISHING
A rudimentary lathe is used in the form
of a large, hand operated wheel which in
turn drives a small wheel by a string. The
metal article is fixed to the spindle of the
small wheel and the article is burnished.

Decorating a bowl in the wax state.

Metal Composition

Bronze and its closely associated metals such as gun metal and bell metal are basically all alloys of copper and tin – with bronze, the copper content is higher usually, 80% of copper and 20% of tin; with gun metal, so named because of its historic use for gun barrels, often 90% copper and 10% tin; bell metal sometimes contains a small amount of silver to improve the ring of the metal. In Kerela the term bell metal is applied to mixtures varying from the highest quality known as Vellodu which is composed of 75% copper and 25% tin, in other words bronze, and is eminently suitable for use as a cooking utensil. Other alloys used for decorative purposes contain copper, tin and zinc – the latter in varying degrees.

Making the first sample of the new range.

110

Design for a candle snuffer.

Sketch book drawing of flower vase.

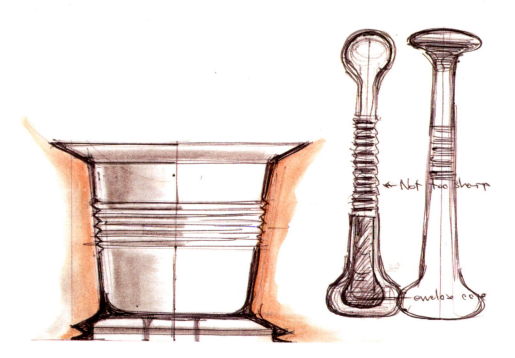

Sketch for pestle and mortar.

← Not too sharp

BRONZE CASTING INDIA 1984

The colour of polished bronze is very pleasing, and for certain functional articles is the most hygienic thing; but it is difficult to stop the gradual loss of polish through oxidisation, and it needs attention from time to time if the lovely colour is to be maintained.

One solution is to patinate the surface and here the colours that can be achieved are legion. Everyone is familiar with the green patina, but beautiful shades of brown, purple etc. can also be achieved;

Bronze pestle and mortar, small mortar, diameter 115mm, large mortar, diameter 120mm.

usually the process involves heating the bronze to a precise temperature and immersing it in a variety of chemicals, a process which often takes days to complete, and when the colour has been achieved, the surface is fixed by an application of beeswax and vigorous polishing.

Ralph Brown is an old friend from Royal College of Art days, who produces beautiful surface treatments on his splendid figurative bronze sculptures. I asked him how I could get a good colour

as an alternative to polishing. He suggested that I worked in conjunction with Kenneth Cook who casts all his bronzes. I asked Kenneth to find an interesting colour that did not need the use of chemicals, which would cause difficulties in the remote Indian workshops. We discussed a variety of solutions, he went away to carry out some experiments and he returned two weeks later with a sample of a beautiful brown, with just a hint of texture on the surface. He had in fact used liquid

elephant dung mixed with turmeric, washed off and left to dry in the sun; a friendly keeper at Bristol Zoo had let him have the essential ingredient. But as things turned out, the craftsmen in India prefer to use less bizarre methods and achieve the patina by using a simple turmeric solution. As the patination experiments continued it became apparent from market research that the coloured finish was greatly preferred and the benefit of developing colour led to the introduction of a bronze chess set.

Looking back, it is difficult to realise that in London in 1954 stainless steel of quality was a metal that had to be searched for – there were only a few retailers in London carrying stainless steel tableware; Heal's had a small display in their basement, mainly of Swedish make, Liberty's had a few showcases, Georg Jensen a small window display in Bond Street and the products of Old Hall, the only British manufacturer of stainless steel of any consequence, could only be found in a few jewellers and silversmiths.

I first became aware of the possibility of designing in stainless steel when I visited Sweden in 1954 and by chance came across a display in a bank window in Stockholm (The Skandinaviska Banken) which showed drawings, dies, models and finished pieces designed by Sigurd Persson and made by the Swedish manufacturer, A. B. Silver & Stal – presumably the window display was to promote the concept of the use of stainless steel, the designer, the manufacturer, and the bank's involvement in the enterprise. At all events, it made a profound impression on me and I became aware of the possibility of undertaking a detailed study of the metal. So, it turned out that my last year at the Royal College of Art, was devoted to stainless steel and I began my researching literally at

TEA SET, VEGETABLE DISH 1954
Until recently it was the practice at the
Royal College of Art to select a few pieces
by departing students for a College
collection; but in 1983 this idea was
abandoned, and past students were given
the opportunity of acquiring their work.
It was a poignant moment for me, to
collect work from which I had been
parted for 30 years or so, particularly the
stainless steel prototypes which are
illustrated on this page, for they were the
forerunners of so much.

All the pieces were made in gilding
metal and finished in a matt satin
chrome, which gave a realistic
impression of satin stainless steel.

the beginning, by spending time in two steel mills in
Sheffield, Firth Brown and Samuel Fox, who both
specialised in making steel. Here I was given every
help and encouragement and most valuable of all,
an introduction to Old Hall who agreed to help in
any way possible on the projects I had planned, some
of which required the use of stainless steel.

My diploma work was an entrée dish with a
removable 3 portion liner and Old Hall bought this
design before I had left college. More designs followed
including a tea set and a condiment set, and when I
left the R.C.A. in the summer of 1955, I had been
engaged by Old Hall to act as their visiting designer,
spending one day a week at their factory, and with the
suggestion that it would be a good idea to establish
my workshop somewhere in the Midlands so that I
could be called upon at short notice if need be; hence
the eventual choice of Chipping Campden.

I was fortunate to arrive at Old Hall at a time
when the great boom for stainless steel was just about
to begin and the directors, with immense courage,
gave me every opportunity and encouragement to
develop new designs; I was appointed Design
Consultant to the company in 1955. My first visit to
the factory in Bloxwich in the autumn of 1954 might

possibly be called auspicious, as I recall that it was some while before I could draw the management's attention to the business in hand, due to the fact that I had arrived in an open 1923 Lancia Lambda. It was not until a few years later that I realised that Lancia cars were an abiding passion for the two brothers, Leslie Wiggin, the Chairman, and Wilfred, the Managing Director.

The Wiggin family of Bloxwich were the very heart and soul of Old Hall Tableware, from the founding of the company in 1904 with the manufacture of stirrups and harness fittings for the Walsall saddlery trade. One of the curious facts about Old Hall is that although its name became synonymous with quality and good functional design, this reputation emerged from a background which was not related to fine tableware and craftsmanship,

Vegetable dish, comprising three separate dishes, made in gilding metal, satin chrome plated.

such as one associated with companies like Elkington, Walker and Hall, and Mappin and Webb.

The first article ever to be manufactured in stainless steel, a toast rack in 1928, is credited to Will Wiggin, one of the founder directors of the company. At that time one of the main lines of the factory was a range of bathroom fittings made originally in chrome plated steel, and later it was also made in stainless steel.

Firth Brown of Sheffield, the steelmakers and producers of Staybrite Stainless Steel, gave Old Hall every support in their efforts to market tableware made in Staybrite; Dr. Hatfield of Firth Brown's laboratory worked closely with Will Wiggin and at the Ideal Homes Exhibition at Olympia, 1934, T. Firth and John Brown jointly sponsored the exhibit, STAYBRITE CITY, and on Old Hall's stand, in pride of place, they exhibited the world's first stainless steel teapot. The close association with Firth Brown continued, and Dr. Hatfield in consultation with Old Hall commissioned a series of designs from the eminent designer, Harold Stabler, R.D.I., and although expensive to make they were elegant and functional designs. However, with the outbreak of war in 1939, the production of stainless steel tableware was abandoned and the factory switched to war work; after the war Old Hall concentrated on overseas markets as it was the only way to obtain a licence to purchase stainless steel.

For two years the export market for stainless steel tableware represented half the turnover of the company until 1953 when the Japanese began to make inroads into Old Hall markets with copies of their teasets. From 1953 onwards the company turned its attention to the rapidly expanding home market.

The first series of my designs to be manufactured was a small collection launched in 1956 which comprised a toast rack, coffee service, condiment set and some dishes, all of which were well received by Old Hall's customers; with a design award for the toast rack in 1958, the stage was set for the next big step, the Oriana Project.

BOAC TABLEWARE 1968
Proposal for a tableware service for First Class passengers, to be used on board the new Jumbo jets that were soon to come into service for BOAC. Only the glassware was manufactured.

Cake knife.

CAKE KNIFE 1953
A fortnight's visit to Sheffield in the
second year was one of the wide range of
activities that formed part of the
excellent course at the Royal College
devised by Professor Goodden, like the
visit to Stourbridge mentioned later.
(Page 186) I made my first pieces of
cutlery in Sheffield in 1953 in the factory
of George Wolstenholme; or rather I
produced the blades with their kind
assistance, and completed the cutlery on
my return to the RCA.

The knife illustrated is made in
stainless steel with a gilt steel tang fitted
inside an acrylic handle.

First design sketch for coffee service, watercolour and ink.

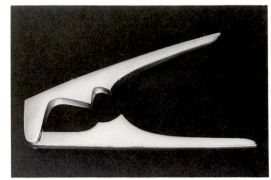

Nutcrackers, 1958.

Campden cutlery.

Components for toast rack.

Toast rack, Design Centre Award, 1958.

A selection of tableware of the late 1950s.

CAMPDEN/SPRING CUTLERY 1956
Old Hall's first venture into cutlery took place just before the Second World War, but nothing came of it. Then, during the early 1950s, the Swedish company Gense made great inroads into world markets, and into Britain in particular, with a very pleasant design called FACETTE. It became obvious that an English design was needed to counter the Gense pattern. The two British companies most likely to meet this challenge were Old Hall Tableware and Walker and Hall of Sheffield, but both seemed reluctant to commit themselves to the cost of producing a new stainless steel pattern.

The matter was finally resolved when the Council of Industrial Design, acting as an intermediary, proposed an amalgamation of the resources of the two companies. Walker and Hall, who had a very active catering and hotel division, would sell the pattern for contract purposes, and Old Hall would handle the retail sales. David Mellor and I, the designers of the respective companies, would collaborate on a joint design project and the actual manufacture would take place in Sheffield; the basic cutlery would then be sent to Old Hall for finishing and polishing.

As things turned out, Walker and Hall made all the cutlery and supplied Old Hall with the finished product; they sold it as SPRING and Old Hall sold it as CAMPDEN. The design sold well, but its split identity was confusing, and from then on Old Hall decided to stick to exclusive patterns.

122

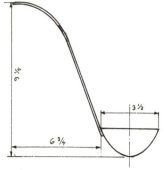

Sauce ladle.

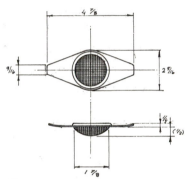

Tea strainer.

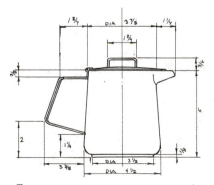

Tea pot.

Sketch to illustrate the versatile design of the ORIANA pots.

A selection of tableware designed for the S.S. ORIANA.

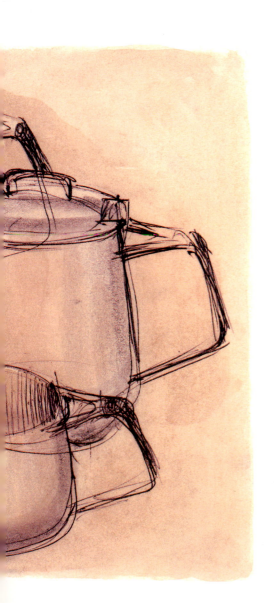

THE S.S. ORIANA 1958-60

One of the most important design commissions I have ever undertaken had its origins in an unlikely introduction. During the 1950s, the London office of Old Hall was run by their agent, Harold Jacobsen, in Fenchurch Street in the City of London. Just around the corner were the offices of the Orient Line, from which Mr. Jacobsen received enquiries from time to time for Old Hall products. In 1956 he had an enquiry for a stainless steel lavatory brush holder – the existing article being far too flimsy for the rough usage on the Orient ships. This enquiry was redirected to my studio and, in close consultation with Phil Robinson, the works manager of Old Hall, we produced a prototype of true battleship strength and quality. The Orient Line Purchasing Department was delighted and Old Hall received a substantial order.

In less than a year I received a personal letter from Mr. Evans, the Director of Supplies for the Orient Line, enquiring if I would be interested in designing tableware for the new liner, S.S. ORIANA, due to be launched in 1960. Several designers had been recommended by the Council of Industrial Design, but in the initial interview, when I referred to my lavatory brush holder, this seemed to inspire confidence and plans were soon discussed to change all the tableware from silverplated nickel silver to stainless steel; with my close association with Old Hall, the only company at that time capable of producing high quality catering ware, the equation fell into place and two years of intense work began.

The problem was divided into two main areas, articles for pouring liquids and containers for serving and presenting food. The first was difficult, especially within the restrictions of the Old Hall tool room. I finally settled on a standard type for the whole range: a simple jug which could be converted into a teapot, coffee pot or ice pitcher by adding components, such as sieve, lid, knob or hinge (see illustration on left).

ALVESTON CUTLERY 1962

The early 1960s were times of major reassessment of everyday objects by designers all over the world, and many areas benefited from the experiments of this period. Furniture design being a prime example with the exciting designs by the Americans, Charles Eames and Harry Bertoria. The early '60s were also the time of many competitions to encourage designers to create the new look, and such a competition was the one held by the International Silver Corporation of Meriden, U.S.A., for the design of new cutlery patterns in silver. The prize money was generous and entries were attracted from many countries.

Condiment set with plastic inserts.

Alveston tea service.

Alveston cutlery, 1962, Design Centre Award, 1964, The British Embassy in the Philippines, 1982.

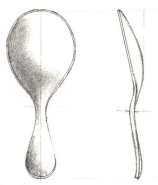

Tea caddy spoon.

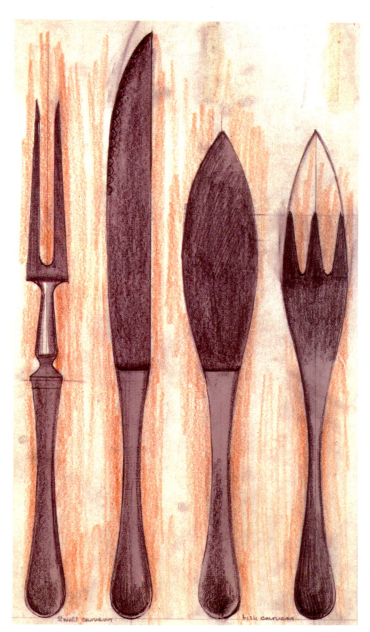

Sketch book drawing of Alveston serving pieces.

I submitted two designs in an experimental manner, and as soon as I sent off my entry I began to feel that I had been self-indulgent; I realised that experiments in other areas had worked well enough, but the same principles did not necessarily apply to cutlery design.

It was as if I had perjured myself with this entry for the competition, and by way of making amends I began working on a new design, later to be known as ALVESTON, which I felt paid due homage to the best traditions of English cutlery.

Alveston must be the only cutlery design that was actually launched at a lecture rather than at a trade exhibition. The Design Council organised a weekend seminar for retailers of cutlery in Sheffield and I was invited to give a lecture on DESIGNING CUTLERY. To complete my review of the cutlery scene in 1963 and to emphasise my quite recent discovery that radical solutions were not valid, I rounded off my lecture by showing slides of the new pattern. The range was officially unveiled at Olympia some months later, in the Watchmaker and Jeweller Exhibition.

It is difficult to realise that since the development of the first brass samples all those years ago, some four million pieces have been manufactured.

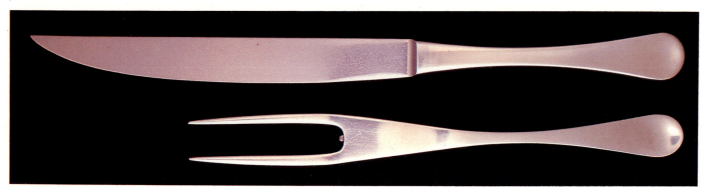

Alveston carving set.

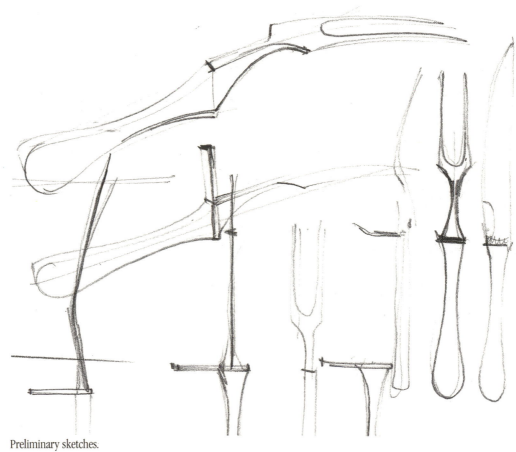

Preliminary sketches.

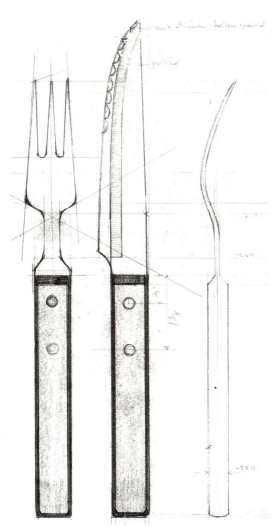

Workshop drawing.

Bistro cutlery with rosewood handles, 1963.

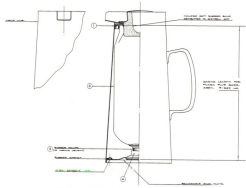

Technical drawing.

Vacuum jug, cream and sugar bowl.

BISTRO CUTLERY & VACUUM JUGS 1959
Examples of the close collaboration that
existed between Old Hall Tableware and
myself in the mid-1960s are illustrated on
this page; neither of these designs were
commissioned by Old Hall, rather they
were the result of proposals for new
products without any brief.

The vacuum jug owed its origin to
Skjalm Petersen's repeated request that I
should make a nice jug that was an
article of tableware rather than the
plastic vacuum jugs which were so
common in Europe in the mid-'70s. The
cutlery owed its origin to Harrison
Fisher who were keen to expand their
own production of kitchen knives by
offering a special range exclusively for
British Home Stores.

The range was designed primarily as
a series of kitchen knives and the steak
knife was developed almost as an after-
thought. However, the project did not
materialise and in collaboration with
Harrison Fisher the idea was developed
into a basic range of cutlery for use in
casual living and offered to Old Hall who
took up the design in 1963. It proved to
be the fore-runner of a new concept of
cutlery which was later to be frequently
copied. At one time I found two identical
versions of this design both from
factories in the Far East.

130

In 1976 Paul Dreyer, Managing Director of Prestige in West Germany, visited the London office of the Prestige Group to discuss possible designs for a new range of kitchen tools; he was going to Japan with the idea of commissioning a new line to be made for the European market.

Lying in a drawer in the product Development Office at Prestige were designs that I had worked on since the early 1970s and which had been abandoned a year or so ago. The idea was a one-piece tool with no visible and unsightly join between the working ends and the handle, which would have been more hygienic than the system used in Prestige's English factory, whereby the two parts were rivetted together. However, the course that was explored to achieve this solution was to attempt to manufacture the tools along the lines of conventional spoon and fork manufacture. In this method a piece of steel is cut out to the general shape required and the working end is thinned down by rolling and the final outline shape is cut, then all the 3-dimensional form is achieved by the pressing in dies.

It subsequently turned out that Mr. Dreyer's visit to Japan was a huge success as the factory he approached with my design, the Kay Cutlery Company, had a brilliant idea to achieve the one piece construction. They proposed making the tools in two parts as the English factory did, but instead of rivetting they introduced a butt weld by using a new system which is used in the aircraft industry. Like all radical departures the idea was simple but it needed great courage to turn this idea into manufacturing reality as the capital involved, both for tooling and the welding plant, was very great.

Eventually in 1977 the tools went into full production and became immensely popular in Europe and Japan. The manufacturing system evolved for this collection, became the norm for quality kitchen tools and was the inspiration for many imitations in the Far East.

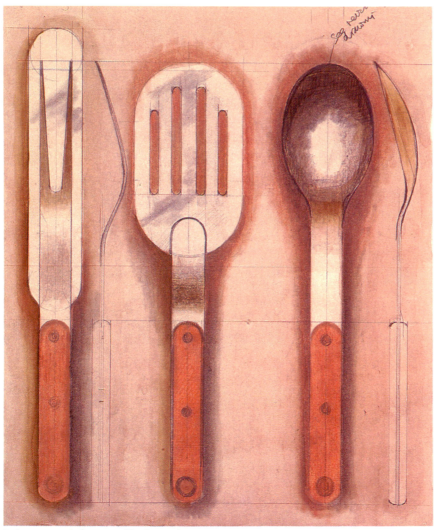

Preliminary study for range of kitchen tools.

Kitchen tools with plastic handles, part of a range of seventeen different designs.

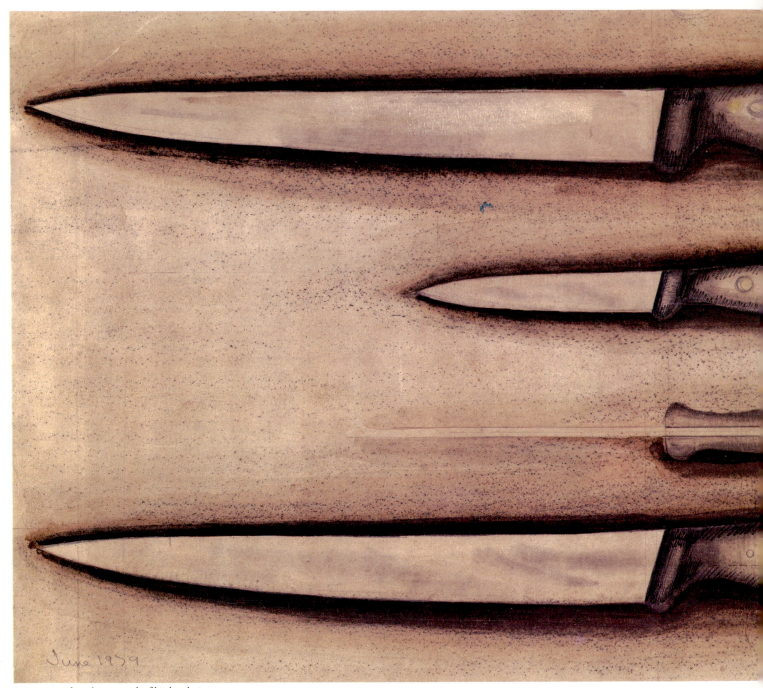

June 1959

Drawing in ink and sepia wash of kitchen knives.

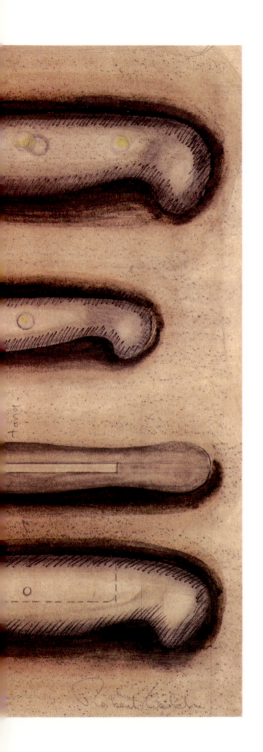

KITCHEN DEVIL KNIVES 1979

As a young man I often visited the Three Counties Show where my father, who worked as sales representative for W. F. Smallman of West Bromwich, a Black Country oil blender, organised and ran their marquee. In the days before the permanent site at Malvern the show moved in rotation between the three counties, Worcestershire, Herefordshire and Gloucestershire. The venues were rudimentary, it always seemed to be raining, and the ground was a quagmire within hours.

In the midst of the confusion of vehicles stuck in the mud and makeshift stalls where salesmen vied with each other, there was always one stand which never failed to attract a large gathering; this was the one where the Bearston cutlery demonstrations took place. The sales pitch was punchy and straight to the point, backed up with an impressive, even awesome, slicing of a soft over-ripe tomato. The farmers and their wives eagerly bought the product; the founder, Harold Bearston had such drive that it is not surprising that he was later able to commission Taylor's Eye-Witness in Sheffield to make his own exclusive design.

Taylor's Eye-Witness had been making Alveston cutlery for four years before Harold Bearston arrived, but it was not long before his product, now known as Kitchen Devil knives, vied with Alveston as the most important line the factory produced. It was also, perhaps, inevitable, that one day Harold Bearston and I should collaborate on a new design programme: this happened in 1979 at the instigation of Roger Inman, the Managing Director of Taylor's Eye-Witness. Having captured the middle market, for kitchen knives in England, it seemed that something should be done about the quality end of this huge business, dominated by foreign manufacturers, particularly Sabatier of France.

The Sheffield management had worked out a revolutionary development route: to mould onto a blade and linish away a section to expose the rear view of the tang, giving the quality look and feel of the hafted handle with a totally hygienic junction and an indestructible union of handle to blade. I developed this idea in my drawings and it is interesting to see that from the earliest sketches the Kitchen Devils' professional concept was quickly established; it required only careful detailing and development to bring the idea into reality.

For Harold Bearston this was a further stage in his plan for a strong British presence in the home market. In 1980 he sold his company to Wilkinson Sword and is now associated with this company. With the financial strength of Wilkinson Sword the sale of Kitchen Devils' products has soared, and in June 1984, the Crown Suppliers decided to refurbish UK Embassies and Consulates with Kitchen Devil Professional knives, instead of a foreign product.

Kitchen knives with plastic handles and brass rivets, Design Centre Award, 1984.

YAMAZAKI CUTLERY

The subtle weaving of threads of chance never cease to amaze me – called the game of connections. If I had never started to make cast iron I could not have counted Skjalm Petersen of Copenhagen as a close friend; if a Dane called Hans Hallundbaek had not resigned as product Development Manager in Japan for Dansk Designs of America and become a consultant with the famous Japanese cutlery factory, Yamazaki, he would not have been in Copenhagen in the autumn of 1979; and if his plans to find designers for the Yamazaki Designers Group and launch of a new company in the USA had not gone astray, he would not have been to see Skjalm Petersen, and I might never have heard of Yamazaki.

Hans Hallundbaek's plan was to commission new cutlery patterns from designers like Henning Koppel of George Jensen, to be made by Yamazaki for the new American subsidiary, but most of the designers he wanted were already under contract. Skjalm telephoned me, and within a few days Hans Hallundbaek was in Chipping Campden. Plans for the new collection were drawn up on the spot.

Design for Dunlop tyre, 1976.

Regalia cutlery.

Drawing in ink and sepia wash for Regalia cutlery.

Regalia serving items.

I had not produced any new cutlery designs for some years, and this was a most welcome opportunity to make a fresh start. In the late 1970s I had been working on a tyre design for Dunlop with particular attention being paid to the new Denovo tyres for the Metro car. The idea was to create a shimmering pattern on the side walls of the tyres by a process of micro-facetting; unfortunately the completed design, although very effective, did not go into production due to the high capital cost of the computerised milling machine required to cut the facets on each individual tyre mould. But I wondered whether I could get an idea for the cutlery out of this project.

It was not the Dunlop design that was used for Yamazaki cutlery but the basic thinking of developing reflecting light from curving flutes and setting these curves on the forks in juxtaposition to the spoons and knives. The pattern that was developed was called REGALIA and it was launched in New York along with other designs in 1980 when the new company, Yamazaki Tableware Incorporated, was officially launched. Since then many more designs have been developed, and the direct relationship between the Japanese factory and myself has grown rapidly, work now being commissioned directly from Japan, both for the American subsidiary and the Japanese home market.

Calibre cutlery, all items have hollow handles.

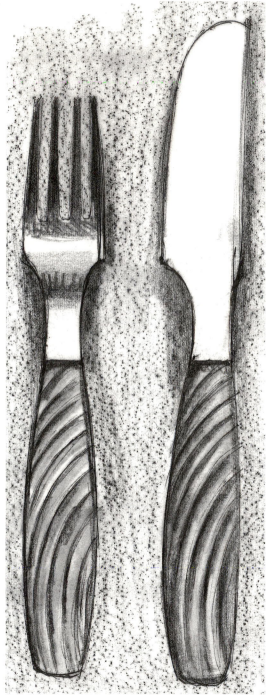

Sketch book drawing.

Beach cutlery with plastic handles.

In 1982 Hans Hallundbaek and his partner, Katherine Vockins, had completed the terms of reference on their consultancy project for Yamazaki and under the dynamic guidance of Etsuji Yamazaki, based mainly at the factory in Japan, the new American management team of Kasy Yawata as vice-president and general manager and Ray Leibman as marketing director, have, in a remarkably short space of time, taken the company to the forefront of the market. Their policy of regularly commissioning designers to produce new ideas has led to their present position as acknowledged leaders of design innovation in this field.

Beach cutlery on its demountable stand.

Beach serving pieces.

Sketch book study.

141

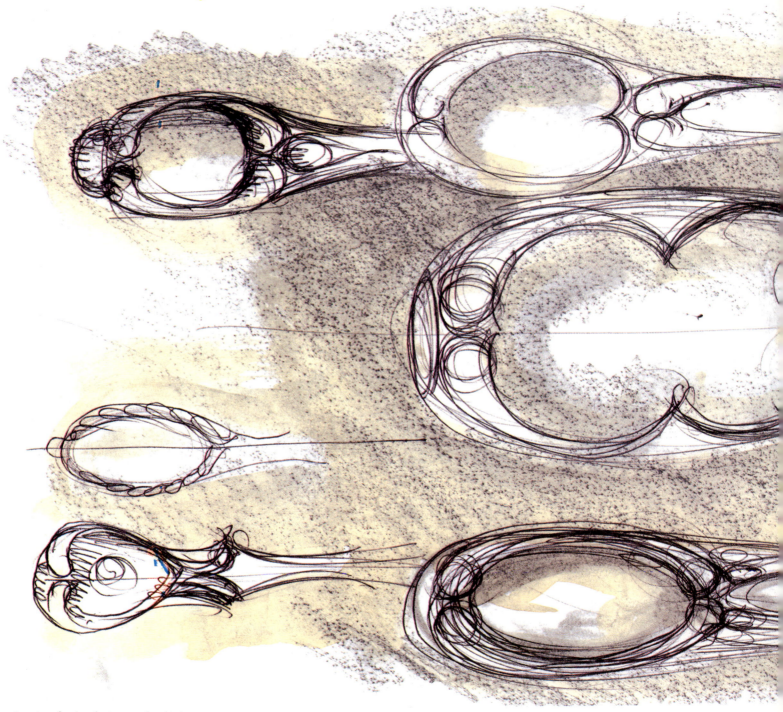

Drawing of cutlery for Japanese hotel industry.

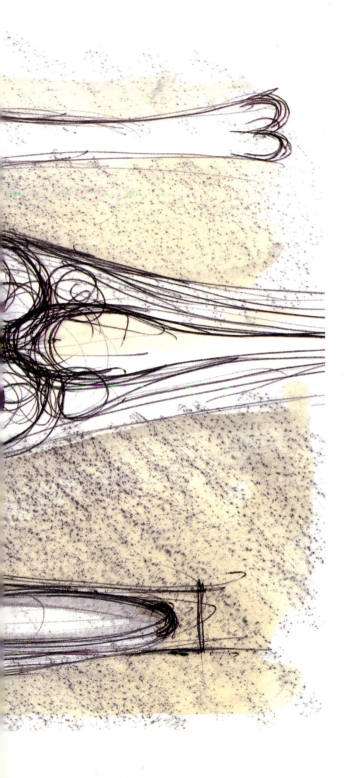

Imperial, silver plated cutlery.

Yamazaki serving collection

First drawing, ink and sepia wash.

YAMAZAKI SERVING COLLECTION 1981-83

When I joined Old Hall Tableware in 1955 as their consultant designer, all the products manufactured by the factory were finished in bright mirror finish, which I felt gave the steel a look that was akin to chrome plate or silver plate.

One of my first tasks was to try to persuade the management to make some designs in a satin finish, which seemed more appropriate to stainless steel. When applied to forms that were simple, if not severe in design, a distinctive character was established. This was in 1955, and it was the beginning in this country of the new look in stainless steel which had already found great favour with the Scandinavian producers, the leading exporters of design in those days. For the next 25 years this finish was to reign supreme as the definitive look for the metal.

The second design, ink and sepia wash.

The third design, ink and sepia wash.

Casserole, ink, charcoal and wash.

Tea kettle, ink, sanquine chalk and wash.

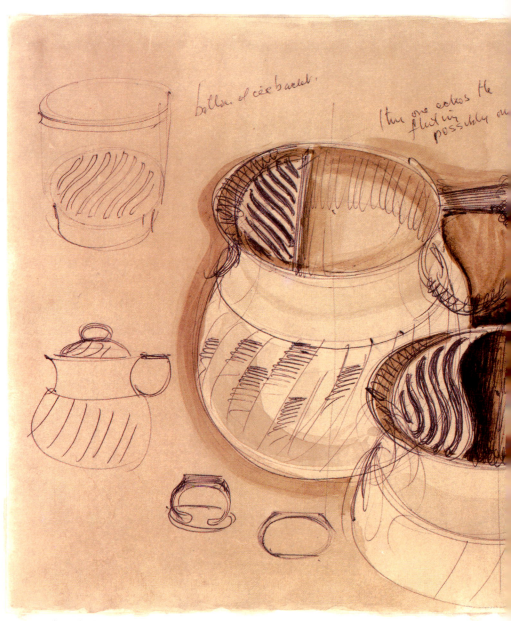

Water pitcher, ink, charcoal, sanquine chalk and sepia wash.

Tea and coffee service.

Unfortunately, what began as an exclusive line, sold in the top quality shops of the day like Woollands of Knightsbridge and Heal's, soon became an avalanche of cheap and shoddy imported imitations. Unlike Old Hall who took immense trouble to achieve a beautiful soft satin finish by polishing the article to a mirror finish and then dulling down to a satin finish, the new imported stainless steel hid a multitude of sins and poor workmanship under a coarse scratched satin surface.

For the quality manufacturers it was a losing battle, satin finished stainless steel had become associated with the imported lines, and few members of the public were prepared to distinguish between the good and the bad.

It was against this background that Yamazaki took the bold decision to enter the American market with a completely new look for stainless steel. In 1981 the metal tableware market throughout the world was in a state of turmoil; silver had been fluctuating wildly due to

148

Sketch book study for the serving collection.

speculators, and it was also at risk because of its value, and a security problem; silverplate was neither fish nor fowl, it needed cleaning and was relatively expensive. What was needed was a brand new look for stainless steel which had nothing to do with severe forms and satin finishes.

The five designers who had worked on the original collection of cutlery were each invited to submit designs for this all-important range. The market was carefully researched and the brief concluded that a transitional look was needed that appealed to the twenty-to-forty age group, but there was still the question of how to breathe new life into stainless steel tableware. The design that was eventually chosen for development emerged in my studio in Campden with

the idea of combining rounded forms with spiral facets, contrasting with plain polished areas; this combination set the style for a development programme.

In 1981 the great test began with drawings and models being shipped between Chipping Campden, New York and Tokyo with bewildering frequency, and gradually the concept took shape. But there were many times when the project seemed still-born; and even when all the production drawings were complete it was not entirely clear how the range would be made. I had one idea, Yamazaki another; furthermore, this was not a venture for the faint-hearted as Yamazaki had decided that if they were to start the programme, all the designs would progress simultaneously; there would be no room for trial and error.

In June 1982 I sent the last details to Japan, and I had then to wait for nine months, wondering just how it would look. After all a wooden model sprayed with silver paint could give no indication of the real effect of the shining, mirror-like forms of polished stainless steel.

At last a telex arrived from Japan telling me to meet a flight at Heathrow. I could hardly contain myself as all the paper formalities had to be dealt with, hopping from foot to foot until I finally received the parcels. I rushed out to the car where I had cutters and knives ready to open the parcels; I balanced ice buckets and jugs on the roof and the bonnet; and I just danced around the car. It was one of the most exciting moments I can remember. Yamazaki had completed a wonderful job.

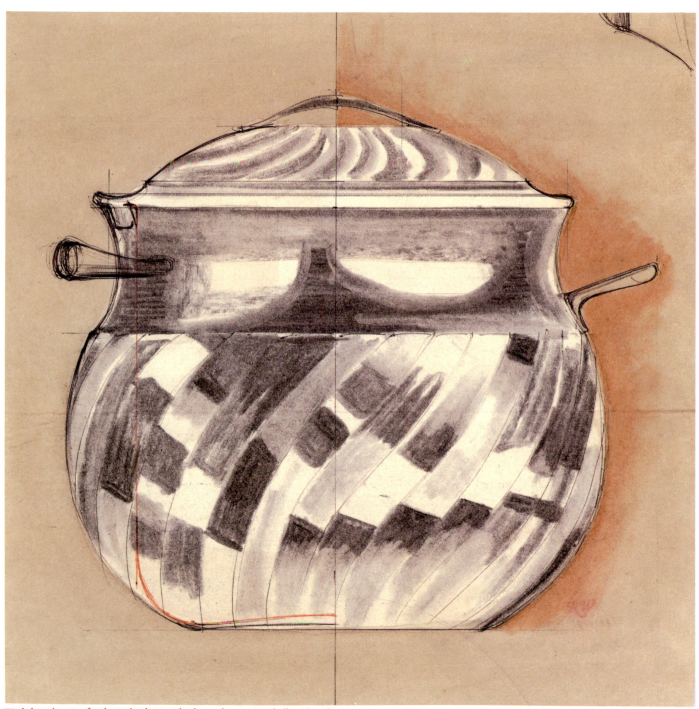

Workshop drawing for the ice bucket in ink, charcoal, sanquine chalk and wash.

KITCHEN TOOLS 1983

When one first encounters the products and literature of catering suppliers, one is brought face to face with a world where aesthetics do not exist; sturdy engineering is the keynote, and robust construction is of prime importance. There is an awesome sense of near-indestructibility; everything is larger and heavier and generally more basic than one is accustomed to in the genteel world of domestic kitchens.

Samuel Groves of Birmingham is a company well known in the catering trade for a wide range of strong utensils and they date back as a firm to the early 19th century when they were brass candlestick makers. Nowadays their reputation depends on their MERMAID catering wares. Their interest in design came about through the rapid growth of the self-service and carvery systems in hotels, restaurants and pubs which have become so popular. With this new way of presenting food, the general public wants other serving tools than those used in the kitchen, as a market survey commissioned by Samuel Groves clearly showed.

Presentation sketch of serving utensils in ink, charcoal and sepia wash.

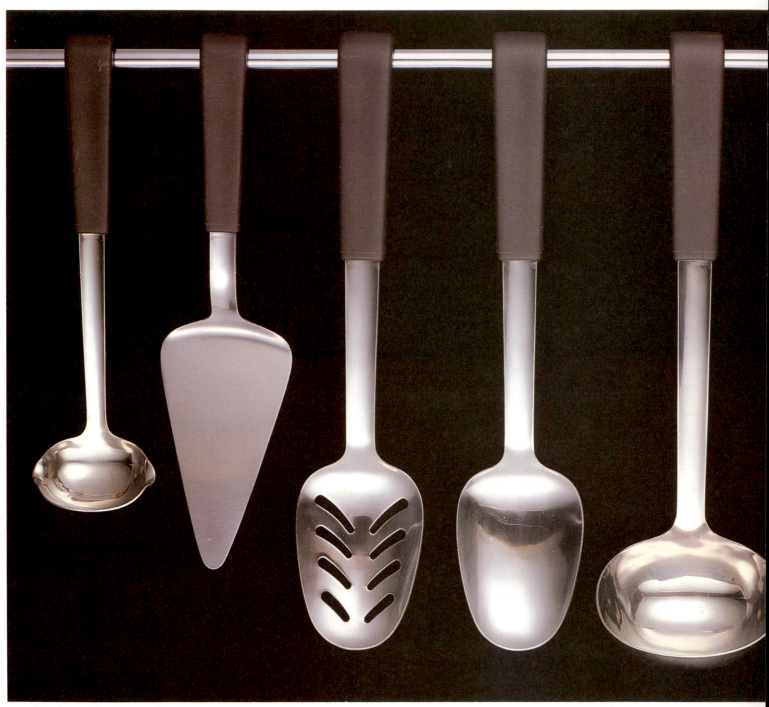

Le Buffet collection of serving utensils.

I was told that the kitchen tools that I had designed for Prestige were sometimes used, but that once behind the beige doors, they were swiftly bent and buckled into unrecognisable shapes in the 'free-for-all' of the professional kitchen. "We need at least double or treble the strength of the Prestige tools," I was told. "The handles must be moulded directly on to the steel and there will be no welding of working ends to handles. The product will be constructed out of one piece of stainless steel and don't forget, they must not bend."

Encouraged by this precise brief and enjoying the opportunity to 'think big', I prepared a sketch for my own purposes of the general direction that should be pursued. As it turned out, the sketch was whisked away and shown to the Board of Samuel Groves and the project was set in motion based on this drawing. The range was launched at Hotelympia in January 1984, and the catering trade showed its approval of the design by an immediate and ongoing flow of orders.

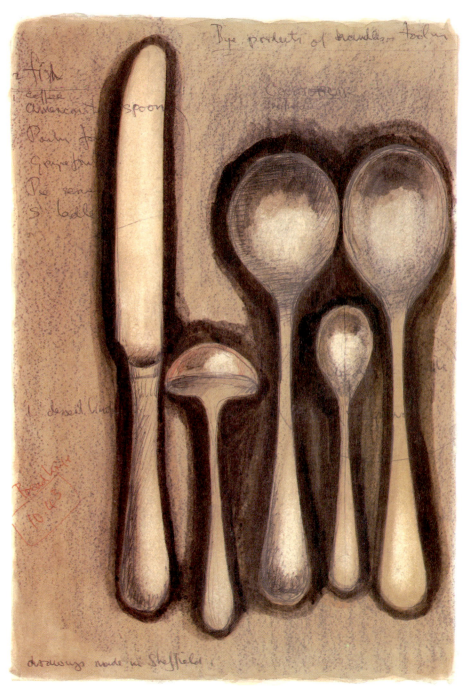

Sketch book drawing for Premier.

COURTIER CUTLERY 1984

The knives belonging to Georgian spoons and forks had blades made of carbon steel which corrodes with the passing of time; and often the handles were made of bone and ivory which again does not last long. Quite often, therefore, people want a knife with a stainless steel blade and a silver handle that will match their antique spoons and forks.

It was to solve this problem that I made the first set of knives for several of my shop customers. They were never intended as a strict match for the old silver pieces, but for using them in the same way that the milk jug I made for J.B. Priestley complemented his Georgian coffee pot, a product of its time rather than a reproduction piece. (See page 28.) Then, from time to time I began to receive enquiries for making spoons and forks to match the knives, and for a long time I wondered about the best way to offer this cutlery at a realistic price. Completely hand-forged spoons and forks are extremely labour intensive and the cost differential between hand-forged and stamped cutlery seems completely out of proportion.

In 1984 the English company, Courtier, well known as a distributor of mainly imported merchandise, decided to commission a new cutlery design to be made in Sheffield. We discussed the direction of the new design, and decided that the work I had already undertaken with my Georgian knives was the correct one and that the new pattern should be as classically English in character as possible – so where better to start than with these knives?

Harrison Fisher were commissioned to undertake the manufacture of the range, and before the pattern was completely tooled up it was submitted for consideration to the Crown Suppliers for the new British Embassy in Riyadh; and it was accepted.

Premier cutlery made in Sheffield by Harrison Fisher Ltd., for Courtier Ltd.

CAST IRON

My interest in cast iron began in 1960 when I was commissioned by a Black Country Foundry to prepare some designs that they could market as their own product. They wanted to offset the uncertainty and fluctuation in the supply of castings to the motor manufacturing industry, so they were looking for a design for a cast iron free-standing ashtray for contract use. The late Peter Cuddon, well known in those days for his fire irons and related metal work, undertook to market the design which unfortunately did not prove successful. However, having studied some of the possibilities of working in this metal I resolved to undertake a personal venture of my own.

If the foundry was worried about the uncertainty of its market I was equally concerned about the haphazard inflow of commissioned silver work and decided that if I could sell a candlestick in silver occasionally, then I could probably sell many more if they were made in cast iron and sold at a very reasonable price. This proved a wise judgement and was the beginning of an exciting venture, which, despite many setbacks and upheavals, still remains a very important part of my design activity.

Since I was trained in silversmithing, I did not find it unduly difficult to come to terms with cast iron. All manner of shapes known as stakes or mandrels which are used in the silver workshop to form and beat silver on, were also made in cast iron; and it was part of one's training in the craft to make patterns in wood and castings in iron – these would be filed to shape and polished before they were put to use.

Within the kitchen cast iron had a long history, cooking ware being the prime example, but it was not so readily accepted as a suitable metal for tableware and it was largely due to my silversmithing background that my first interest was in articles of a decorative nature. This was also my very first venture into batch production. I had simply no idea of how to sell a product to a shop – selling to friends had been easy, but now my problems were about to begin.

From the first candlestick, the range was expanded rapidly to form a small family of related shapes, a pre-requisite for being able to offer the concept as a viable collection.

Interest from export markets was immediate and the second design I made, a fruit bowl, was illustrated in the STUDIO YEAR BOOK OF DECORATIVE ART. This brought a letter from Skjalm Petersen in Denmark ordering thirty-six bowls with no mention of the price, indeed the piece only existed as a sample.

COMMEMORATIVE BOX 1977
This box was commissioned by The Ironbridge Museum to commemorate the 200th anniversary of the building of the Iron Bridge. 76mm x 107mm.

I decided, not unreasonably, that if orders like this were to be had in Denmark, then I should undertake an immediate trip to find out more about the Scandinavian markets. I visited Norway, Finland, Sweden and Denmark armed with some samples and met with little success until I eventually arrived at Skjalm Petersen's shop in Copenhagen. Our meeting was very cordial and he confirmed his order for the fruit bowl plus a very large order for other pieces – this began a close and fruitful collaboration that has lasted to this day.

The impetus for a major development of cast iron came from America. I had for a number of years exported various items in this range to Georg Jensen Inc. of New York, and it was through this association that H. E. Lauffer Co. Inc. commissioned the design of a range of cast iron cookware, which was originally to be manufactured in the U.S.A., but this proved impracticable and the collection was manufactured from 1971 onwards in England. It was, however, another fourteen years, before the decorative range of cast iron and the cookware were to be unified and marketed as a cast iron collection by Victor Cast Ware.

Fruit bowls.

Nutcracker.

Fruit bowls, diameter 255mm.

Pepper and Salt mills.

EARLY DAYS 1962
I can clearly remember my first thoughts when I decided to experiment with cast iron as a possible material for tableware. The candlestick illustrated was the first design I produced which led to the development of this family of shapes. The curved flanged forms of the candlestick of 1962 proved to be a very enduring concept capable of a wide variety of applications which formed a large range of related pieces.

Candlesticks in three different sizes.

Oval casserole from a range of eighteen related shapes.

COOKWARE 1971
I have never met Sigurd Persson, the Swedish designer, but his stainless steel had on a profound effect me in 1953; and strangely our paths crossed briefly again. He had designed a range of cast iron cookware for a Swedish company called Ronproducta which supplied the Swedish chain of Co-operative stores with the range. Uno Berg, the owner of the company, had it cast in England by Qualcast, shipped to Sweden, where the bases were machined, and then sent straight to the Co-operative stores as raw cast iron which had to be oiled and 'broken in' by the customers.

Originally all cast iron was made like this and it is supposed to be very healthy as the food absorbs a certain amount of iron, though problems can arise with rusting. Cast iron is perfect for use with oils and fats, casseroles and frying pans building up an ever-improving, and eventually non-stick, surface.

During 1977, I took over and marketed my Lauffer collection of cast iron with a vitreous enamelled finish. There were technical problems at the foundry and it was difficult, if not impossible, to achieve a perfect enamelled surface; so I began to explore alternative finishes, particularly an oiled finish that accelerated the breaking in process, which is very time consuming.

But I could not achieve the results I wanted, until one day at Kinver Glass Works, run by my old friend, Mike Davies, I noticed a long oven with a slow conveyor belt that took two hours to

Cookware, barbeque grill and chicken fryer.

Cast iron cookware.

Casseroles

travel the full length. Mike said I could try an experiment with a piece of cast iron. I bought some vegetable oil, wiped the iron all over, placed it in the oven and when the iron came out it was battleship grey. Yet another failure, I thought, as I wiped it but the surface came up a brilliant shining black. I carried out tests and this finish was permanent. I immediately made arrangements with Mike to use his oven at slack periods.

The very first day when a trial batch of some 50 castings were passed through the oven disaster struck. A casserole lid that had been incorrectly placed toppled over; the oven could not be stopped and the entire contents of glass and cast iron moved slowly down to the blockage and broke up on the lodged casserole with a long and sickening crash. Nothing could be done until the oven was stopped and cooled off and the shattered glass removed; faces were either ashen or very red. I told Mike that from then on I would stick to vitreous enamelling and he agreed!

Tape dispenser in a variety of colours, length 155mm.

Pestle and mortar, diameter 105mm.

COMMISSIONS 1963 ONWARDS

In about 1963 I had the idea of making a very large iron candlestick, so big and heavy that it could just be handled by one person; it held a huge candle such as one occasionally sees used in cathedrals.

Eric Talbot of Wigmore Distributors, who was selling my range of cast iron at that time, would take this candlestick to exhibitions as a show-piece. At one show he was pleased to receive an enquiry from an American visitor who expressed his interest in acquiring a large candlestick. Eric was delighted and pointed to the exhibition piece. "No," said the American, "That won't do, I want a really large candlestick." From that moment the large candlestick lost its jumbo classification. There was however, an unforeseen aspect to the making of such pieces, for it led to a number of commissions for special 'one-offs' which continued with varying degrees of activity ever since. In these pieces, the materials used have varied, but the technique has remained the same.

Trivet fitted with rubber feet, 135mm x 210mm.

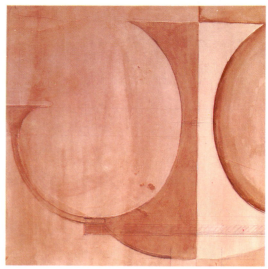

Pencil and sepia wash sketch for chandelier.

Cast aluminium font, Rutgers Church, Pennsylvania, U.S.A.

The Font for Rutgers University in the U.S.A. and the chandeliers for Browne's Hospital, Stamford, were both made of cast aluminium. Annually since 1965 there have been wall plaques made for the Royal Institute of British Architects, Housing Design plaques, and many others, including special 'one-off' designs like the Snell Bridge plaque for Balliol College, Oxford. All these plaques have been cast in bronze from patterns made in my workshop by John Limbrey.

The largest pieces I have designed were the 'Torcheres' for the Mid-Warwickshire Crematorium. They stood over 5 feet high, but because of their size and weight it was necessary to cast them in aluminium. The crematorium was opened in 1972; it is a fine modern building in a beautiful woodland setting; one chapel is square in plan, the other octagonal, and I made the design of the candlesticks on a square and an octagonal plan, to match each chapel.

All these commissions have been cast at the foundry of Ball Brothers Limited.

Cast aluminium chandelier which incorporates two electric light fittings, diameter 760mm.

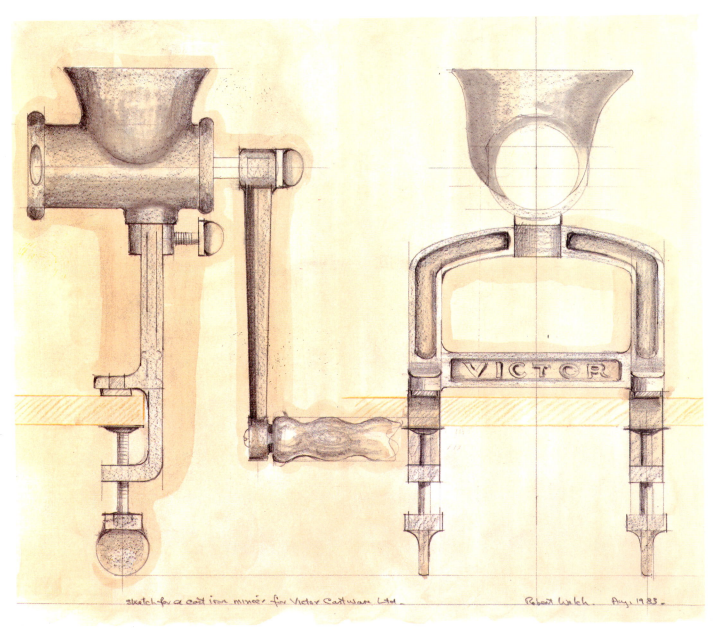

sketch for a cast iron mincer for Victor Castware Ltd.   Robert Welch.   Aug. 1983.

Coffee grinder, pencil and sepia wash.

Coffee grinder.

Sketch book note for metric weights.

CAST IRON 1983

After years of fluctuating fortunes my range of decorative cast iron ware was in a sorry state; it was certainly loved by the few, who struggled to keep it going, but the patient needed a permanent oxygen supply lest it expire altogether!

The collection was still being made by Victor Castings, but there had been all manner of setbacks in production, and it was only made in very small quantities, and my shop in Chipping Campden was one of the main outlets.

Sketch book note for metric weights.

Sent to V.C.

14-1-83

Rough sketches for scales and weights.

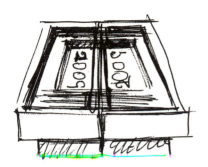

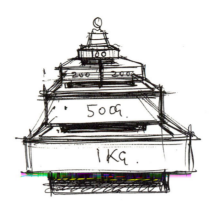

Then one day in the Autumn of 1981 their Managing Director, Paul Richards, went to a gymkhana where his daughter was riding, and began talking to a fellow spectator. The conversation gradually turned to Paul's association with cast iron castings, and he happened to mention the decorative collection. His companion was involved with the Ironbridge Gorge Museum, and already interested, he now became very interested indeed. He made an appointment there and then to visit the factory and find out more.

Set of weights and cast iron scales.

This was how Bob Scott, the brilliant entrepreneur and founder of Scotcade, became involved in the venture. With characteristic incisiveness, he acted swiftly; it was just the direction he wished to develop, as recently he had sold Scotcade to Courtaulds and was looking for a new and exciting challenge. With his colleague from Scotcade days, Derek Griffiths, the Victor Company was restructured and a new era began. Within two years the turnover has soared and instead of two people undertaking the assembly there are now already 25 new jobs created.

Today, when I visit the factory near Telford and watch the thousands of castings being processed, I think back to those early struggling days of 1962 as we assembled peppermills in the Campden workshop and I would set off to sell the pieces packed in suitcases. It has been a long process, full of excitement and disappointments, and now the project has reached a stage that could not have been foreseen in 1962.

Scales in ink, charcoal and wash.

INDUSTRIAL DESIGN

A letter from Christine Foyle in the autumn of 1955 marked the beginning of my introduction to product design. In this letter she said that she had seen my work in the STUDIO YEAR BOOK OF DECORATIVE ART for 1955, and asked if I would be interested in having an exhibition at Foyles Art Gallery in the following year.

I worked very hard towards the preparation of this show in silver and stainless steel, and in September 1956 it opened. The exhibition comprised mainly the work that I had completed at the Royal College of Art, with the addition of a few more recent silver commissions, some small pieces of domestic silver that I made specially for the occasion and the first products manufactured by Old Hall Tableware.

I shared the gallery, which was situated on the top floor of Foyles' Bookshop, with a painter, whom, it transpired, was a friend of Lady Edwina Mountbatten. I spent most of my days during the period of the exhibition at the gallery, but few visitors came, nor did the eagerly awaited orders materialise, until one memorable day, Lady Mountbatten called to see her friend's paintings and, having purchased a selection, she then looked at my work and bought the pieces of domestic silver that I had made for the show. Later, on the same day, a gentleman asked me to tell him about

GUINNESS 1964
To design beer pumps for Guinness you need the constitution of an ox. Soon after I arrived at their headquarters in Dublin I was told that a visit to a special research department was called for. I followed my host expecting to be shown the technical aspects of drawing Guinness under laboratory conditions. Instead I was shown a long bar with pumps of all sizes and shapes, mounted at regular intervals.

My host began with the nearest pump and drew a foaming pint which he placed on the bar, explaining the pump's shortcomings. Then he continued down the bar until there were some fourteen pints in a row.

I need not have wondered what was to happen next. "Cheers" he said, and began to consume them in swift gulps. "Come along, you must sample real Guinness; it won't taste like this in England." Day one of market research faded into the vague memories of smiling faces behind foaming heads of jet black liquid.

My eventual design represented a glass of Guinness made in plastic, with a mirror-finished dome in stainless steel for the head of the beer. It was not accepted by the company.

the stainless steel products on show – he seemed very interested and introduced himself as Mr. Halliwell, Head of the School of Industrial Design at the Central School of Arts and Crafts. He asked me if I would consider a post as a visiting lecturer in the school and run a course on stainless steel design; this was an opportunity which I jumped at, and it came about that after so many years devoted to silversmithing, I was to spend the years 1957 to 1962 on a one-day a week basis, among the industrial designers. I tried to give them an awareness of craft allied to production and they in turn brought me into close contact with the world of product design.

I would like to think in retrospect that it was a fruitful collaboration, certainly every help was given to me by all the staff and one thing I will always remember with pleasure and gratitude, was the way the silversmithing school liaised with my group of industrial designers, by offering them full facilities of their workshop while they were under my charge.

As a first year project we entered the first set of exercises in the annual Goldsmiths' and Silversmiths' Competition of 1957, and several pieces were commended and one received a prize. The whole group of pieces were subsequently shown at various exhibitions at Goldsmiths' Hall and illustrated in a review of Modern Silver published in 1959 by the Worshipful Company of Goldsmiths. The young product designers were delighted with the recognition that their work received, and were particularly pleased to be making pieces which were usable items that they could keep, rather than the scale models or mock-ups which were the norm of the school.

It was at the Central School in the late 1950s, while working with the product designers, that the idea of trying to blend relevant elements from the silversmith and industrial designer into a specific course occurred to me as a possible plan for a future way of training the craft-based product designer. It seemed clear to me then, and still does today, that there is a very real need for such a training.

In 1962 when I left the Central School and began a similar appointment in the School of Silversmithing at the Royal College of Art, it seemed possible to develop this idea. A course of technical drawing was started and students were encouraged to undertake production projects, but gradually at first, and then with ever increasing momentum, the students turned their attention to the fine art aspect of their craft; this was, after all, the middle '60s, and it seemed that the

178

affluent society was here to stay. In retrospect, it was perhaps inevitable that this should be the direction for the next decade or more. The cult of the gallery show, the exhibitions, and the impetus given to the crafts by the foundation of the Crafts Council, from the early '70s onwards, directed the attention of most of the young aspiring craft designers towards a world based on the concept of the craftsman as an artist. It seemed to me that the gap between work of that kind, and offering beautifully designed everyday objects at prices most people could afford, remained as large as ever; and, as Sir Gordon Russell once said to me towards the end of his life, "When I look in the High Street shops I can see no change in design values at all; it seems that all my efforts have been in vain."

But to return to the situation in my workshop in the late '50s and early '60s, silver commissions, the original mainstay of my workshop, remained spasmodic and erratic, whereas there did appear to be a plentiful supply of industrial design projects – furthermore, there were comparatively few practising industrial designers to handle this work.

Old Hall Tableware was already manufacturing a number of my designs in stainless steel and the Scottish clock factory, Westclox, was offering commissions to various designers through the Council of Industrial Design recommendations. In 1958 I had the good fortune to have one of my design proposals accepted by Westclox and this soon led to a long-term contract which lasted until the end of the 1960s.

This was a period, when, for me, product design expanded far more rapidly than I could ever have hoped for and soon included bone chinaware for A.T. Finney, ceramic washbasins for Doulton, work for Guinness on beer pumps, lavatories and washbasins for British Rail, door furniture for Dryad and many more commissions. The work load was very great and I required extra help; John Limbrey had joined me in 1958 and in 1960, one of my students from the Central School, John Wickham, joined the studio for two years, largely to help with the Westclox programme. He made an important contribution to the expansion of Industrial Design in broad terms and in particular with various projects for Westclox.

When John Wickham left, his place was taken by Neville Morgan, a designer trained at the Royal College of Art, and although work for Westclox and other industrial concerns continued, there was a gradual decline of new commissions. A change of management at Westclox rather curtailed the impetus

DOULTON WASHBASIN 1959
Washbasin manufactured by Doulton in vitreous glazed earthenware, designed in conjunction with Doulton's staff designer.

of new design work and when Neville Morgan departed in 1965 John Limbrey took over the combined roles of design assistant, modelmaker and silversmith – a position which he still holds.

By the mid-1960s, it was difficult to distinguish the right route between two possible avenues that both seemed to beckon – there was, on the one hand, the possibility of expanding the Industrial Design side and on the other, the development of the silversmithing side into a larger unit. During this period many young assistants were employed on a temporary basis, varying their stay from summer vacations to several years, to develop models or make silverware.

The question was gradually resolved when, in 1969, I opened the Studio Shop in Chipping Campden. The silversmithing side from then onwards relied less on special commissions and the range of domestic ware rapidly developed and product design became of far greater interest to me if the end result was a design that could eventually be sold in the shop.

Dryad has been a name to reckon with in the history of British design in the 20th century. The firm was founded more than seventy years ago by Harry Peach, an influential figure; and Dryad Metal Works was established in 1926 with W. H. Pick as the chief metalworker. Roger Peach was responsible for design from the 1930s until his death in 1964. He was the son of the founder and won a design centre award in 1957.

It was in the mid-1960s that Peter Ashberry, his successor, came to me to discuss designs for high quality door furniture. There is a peculiar problem in this kind of work, which is that tiny pin holes develop in the castings; during manufacturing these are almost invisible, but when the castings are anodised they show up as unsightly blemishes. We discussed the problem for a long time before deciding to take a quite new approach. We chose to base the designs on aluminium extrusions which are limiting from a design point of view

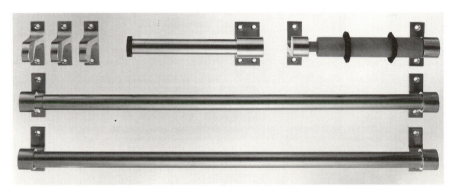

Door furniture in aluminium for Dryad Ltd.

Chantry knife sharpener, 1964.

because the form is always governed by the section, but they provide a surface that is perfect for finishing.

As it turned out, the idea of making a wide range of designs from a single extrusion worked very well and from this shape it proved possible to make coat hooks, toilet roll holders, towel-rails, soap dishes and a whole variety of specialised designs.

The great advantage of being able to produce so many different designs from a stock extrusion was that any of these

designs could be manufactured at relatively short notice and if necessary in small production batches. This was a great advantage in the 1960s when there were often difficulties in obtaining supplies of raw materials such as castings and forgings.

The Dryad 70 range as it was called was conceived during the mid-60s and remained in production until the early 80s, when labour costs had become so critical that the conversion of extrusions was no longer a viable technique.

Merlin alarm clock, made by Westclox Ltd., Design Centre Award, 1964.

I can still see today traces of the clocks we designed in the early '60s for Westclox, although few people would recognise them, the design of clock faces changes so quickly.

There are two distinct areas in clock design; the long-term side of the problem is the design of the case and general assembly of the clock; the short-term aspect is the design of dials and hands. It is these which are of primary concern in the market place, and it is rare for a clock to be designed in which the case and the face remain united for long.

In 1960 Colin Forbes and Alan Fletcher designed my letterhead and I was so impressed that I persuaded them to put forward ideas to Westclox for some dial designs for a new alarm clock that was about to be launched. The presentation took place in 1963 at Crawford Mews, in the new office of Fletcher Forbes and Gill; "Alas, too far ahead of their time." was the verdict of the Westclox management. The present-ation models were packed up in a box, returned to Campden, and forgotten.

At my Campden workshop there is a large attic which is the usual last resting place for all those designs and projects that have been still-born, as well as the first tentative trial models for objects that have ultimately been successful. It is part Aladdin's cave, and part a huge junk store. It was during a recent search of the attic that the Fletcher Forbes and Gill clock faces came to light and here they are, illustrated for the first time.

Merlin clock face designed by Fletcher Forbes & Gill, 1962.

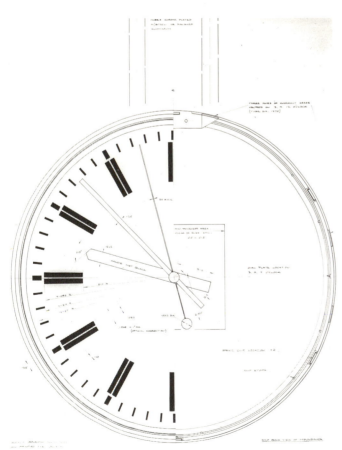

Wall clock for the Ministry of Works and Public Buildings.

Enamel steel kettle for Carl Prinz A.G., Western Germany.

CARL PRINZ A.G. 1965-68
I started working for Carl Prinz of Solingen in the mid-'60s when West Germany's economic miracle was in full swing: inflation and recession were unknown, production and sales graphs pointed upwards only, and it looked as if things would remain that way for ever.

Carl Prinz produced enamelware under the dynamic directorship of Eric Ullendahl, who knew that the best way to sell in England was to employ an English designer. So here I was attending sales meetings with representatives not only from Germany but from all over Europe, discussing how the Swiss like their cheese fondue cooked, and the way bouillabaisse is served in Marseilles.

The sheer size and variety of the European market, and of West Germany in particular, was astounding, and I would go back to Old Hall and try and persuade them to create designs for export; but the British home market was buoyant and required all their attention thus remaining their sole object.

Old Hall and Carl Prinz represented two different kinds of marketing philosophy. When I began working for Yamazaki in Japan in 1979 I discovered another. Old Hall sold 90% of their products in the U.K.; Yamazaki exported 90% of theirs. By the mid-'70s, Carl Prinz had closed down all their cutlery factories; and in 1984 Old Hall ceased trading altogether. Many factors contributed to these changes, but the lesson of Yamazaki's dynamic export orientated marketing policy is unavoidable.

LEAD CRYSTAL GLASS 1953

When I was at the Royal College Robert Goodden was the Professor of Siver-smithing, and a most sensitive and helpful teacher he was too. His philosophy was to leave his students pretty much alone on a day-to-day basis, so that varying talents worked and reacted on each other, and together they simmered in a gentle stew with only an occasional stir from the Professor, aided by a number of firm directions that he had established. One of these was a two-week visit to Stourbridge College of Art to study glass-making, under Mr. Stainer Sr., a brilliant master-craftsman who was a resident demonstrator at the College.

Everyone would look forward to the visit to Stourbridge, and would come back with samples of glass designed and

Museum Study, 1968.

Sketch for lead crystal, 1953.

made on the spot, an exciting experience after the long and laborious process of making pieces of silverware.

David Mellor made some fine condiment sets which he mounted with silver, and Gerald Benney surprised everyone by taking with him a large brass pot he had made with vertical slots pierced all around the side walls, and returned with the glass bulging through the slots. He had Mr. Stainer take a large gathering of glass and blow it directly into his pot, which acted as a mould.

Robert Goodden had himself designed some excellent mass-produced glassware for Chance Brothers, which ought to be collectors' items now. I remember the few weeks I spent at Stourbridge as if it were yesterday, so greatly did I enjoy the experience. And then, in 1969, I finally got a chance to work in glass, when Old Hall acquired the Bridge Crystal Glass Company of Stourbridge. The goblets illustrated on this page are part of a range that has been made in batch production since that time.

Lead crystal goblets.

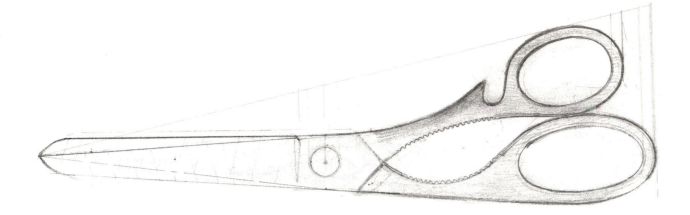

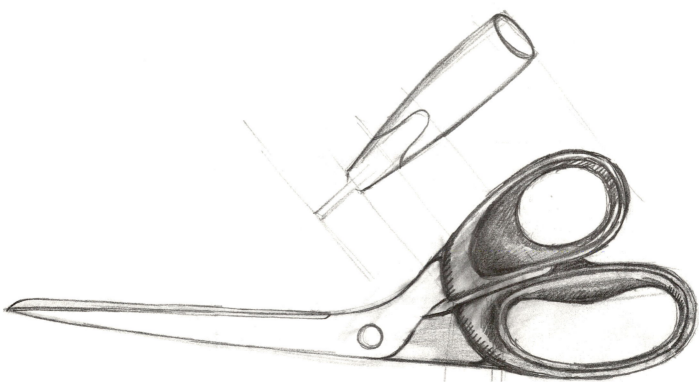

Design sketch for scissors.

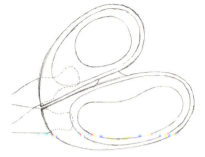

HARRISON FISHER 1964 ONWARDS

The two factories with whom I have enjoyed the longest and closest association are Old Hall at Bloxwich, now sadly no more, and Harrison Fisher of Sheffield. For 22 years these companies worked closely together, and I have worked independently for both.

Harrison Fisher has continued to prosper in spite of the difficult economic climate when nearly all their Sheffield rivals have ceased trading. The reason for their success has been the wise management of Roger Inman and William Fisher who steadfastly pursued a policy of great diversification and wide variety of products; they have actually made most of the Old Hall cutlery designs; then, under their trade name of Taylor's Eye-Witness, they make the Kitchen Devil collection of household and professional knives; and they also make knives, pen knives, and scissors for every purpose under the name of Harrison Fisher, and the various models of the Chantry Knife Sharpeners.

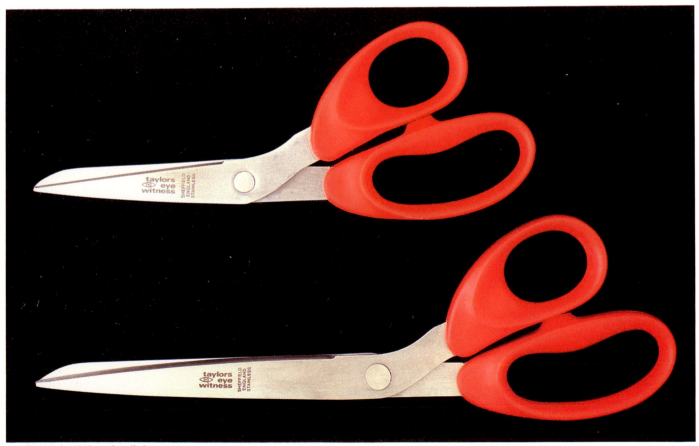

Stainless steel and plastic handled scissors.

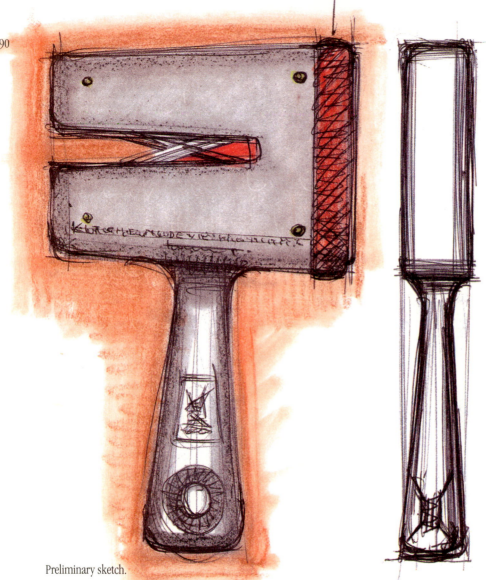

Preliminary sketch.

To visit their splendid late 19th century factory is indeed an education: it is a perfect and harmonious combination of the old and the new, and embodies all the virtues expounded by companies like Volvo of Sweden – the value of the small team operating in its own individual workshop environment, – the feeling of intimacy and fellowship with which no modern factory layout can compete. The workshops which collectively comprise the factory exude a spirit of fine craftmanship which is indefinable but unmistakable. There seems to be something special in the ambience of the buildings; the old Mill in Campden has the same quality.

The company itself is a combination of many famous Sheffield names, which are used for trading and are still well known today, including Taylor's Eye-Witness, founded in 1830, and Chantry and Sanderson; and of famous names of a bygone age like Tyzack, Needham.

Now the two sons of the next generation of the families of Roger Inman and William Fisher are taking the company forward and amongst their many newest projects is a cutlery programme for Marks and Spencer's, and a high quality stainless steel pattern for the English distributor, Courtier.

Knife sharpener in nylon, made in a variety of colours.

LUMITRON 1966

The ramifications of my cast iron venture seem endless. My arms were aching from carrying what seemed to be hundreds of candlesticks into Heal's one day, and I jokingly complained to my old friend, Rolf Falk, that I could not go on like this. "Well, why don't you get yourself a distributor?" he said. "Go and have a word with Eric Talbot at Wigmore Distributors – he might be interested in handling the line." So I walked into Eric Talbot's small showroom in Chiltern Street – just as he was cutting his birthday cake, as it happens – and introduced myself. He agreed to act as distributor and with great relief, I returned to my role of silversmith, design and prototype development.

Our association continued for many years, beginning in 1963, and it was through Eric that I met Carl Prinz and became their designer, and through Eric's partner, Terry Scully, that I was introduced to a small company, Lumitron, who specialised in contract lighting for architectural purposes. They asked me to submit designs; I had very little experience of work in this field, but somehow my Lumitron idea worked. I have never known a design concept appear, as this one did, in the proverbial flash of inspiration; it fell into place as if it were pre-ordained, and not just one lamp but a series of different types, each closely related to one another.

The first model of 1964, a table lamp, was made up in brass and I still have this lamp today. There were no dimensional changes either to this lamp or to any other in the range.

Lumitron have developed considerably and are now one of the larger suppliers of contract lighting in the U.K., and part of the Associated Newspapers Group. The lamp, meanwhile, has quietly lodged itself in the national consciousness. Somehow it seemed to appeal to television designers, and for a time it was a standard feature of the sets for Morecambe and Wise, and any number of chat shows.

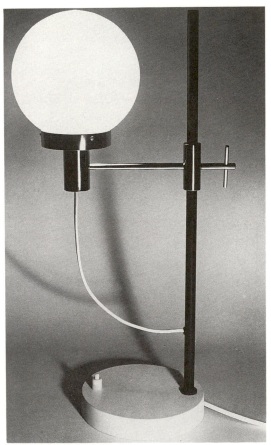

Prototype lamp for Francis Mackmin Ltd., 1958.

Acrylic lamps from a range of eight related designs.

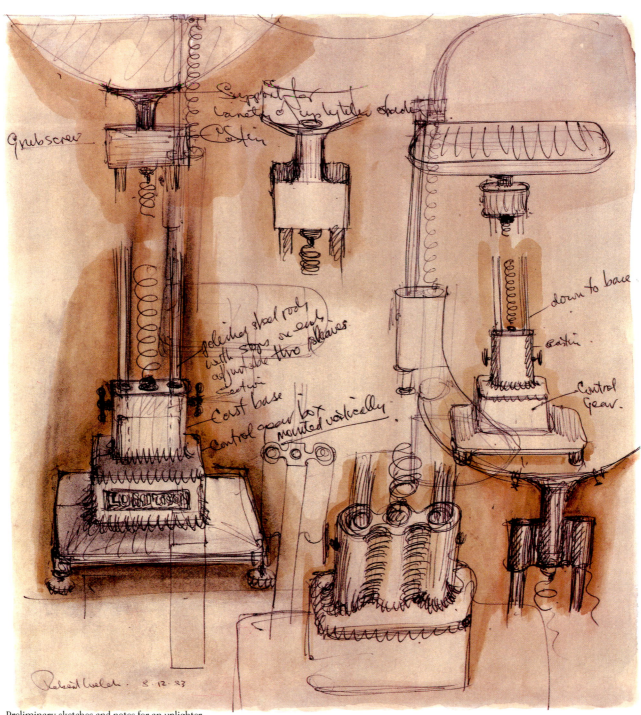

Preliminary sketches and notes for an uplighter.

NEW LUMITRON LAMP 1984

Reflected light as opposed to direct light gives a pleasing overall illumination in an interior. It is a technique that has been in use since the invention of electric light bulbs and was used by the designers of the 1930s to very good effect.

In recent times new powerful light sources have introduced further possibilities for developing this type of lighting and which has proved particularly applicable for use in open plan offices especially where there are operators working in front of V.D.U. screens. The light reflected from a source like sodium discharge creates a restful, warm and non reflective light, ideal for this type of activity.

The design brief from Lumitron was to create a light that blended unobtrusively into all types of interiors, classically simple in design and capable of achieving an excellent light spread.

The fitting is quite large, the transformer and choke are mounted in the base and the large sodium discharge lamp is mounted horizontally in the specially formed shade which was the key to the overall concept of the design.

The drawings on the left are preliminary studies produced before the sodium discharge equipment was available for detailed measurements to be made. Although the final design appears to be simple in form it was the result of a year's work and many full sized models were made before it was finally accepted for production. Matching wall mounted lamps will complete the programme during 1985.

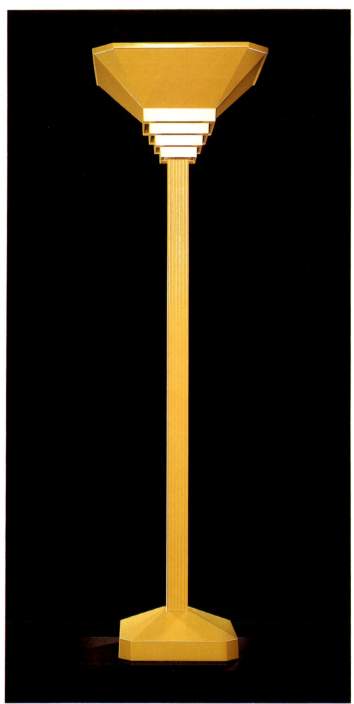

Uplighter in plastic and extruded aluminium, height 1750mm.

Kettle in stainless steel and plastic for A/S Wejra, Denmark.

WEJRA DENMARK 1974

The Danish Company, Wejra, are the largest manufacturer of mortar shell cases in Scandinavia, and when they thought of diversifying into stainless steel cookware they contacted me through Skjalm Petersen.

In 1974 I designed a stainless steel kettle for them which remained in production for about eight years, but the recession put an end to the entire line of cookware experiment.

It was beautifully made, with a thick machined copper plate welded to the base. It seems to have become a collector's item recently: I put the last kettle that I had in stock on show in my shop, really as an archive sample, and priced it at £60 to deter anyone from buying it. But it was quickly sold!

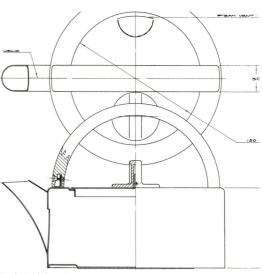

Technical drawing.

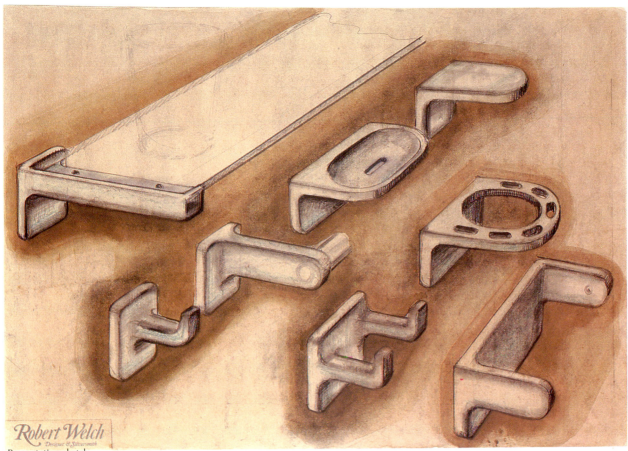

Presentation sketch.

BATHROOM FITTINGS 1976

Adie and Nephew are the largest manufacturer of bicycle bells in England, but in the mid-1970s, Andrew Evans, the Managing Director, felt that they should diversify and he had the idea of a new range of bathroom fittings.

I shall never forget how he told me about it. He is an enthusiastic rock climber and we were on Snowdon. I had never been climbing before (or since), and was appalled at the so-called 'safe area' from which he pulled me on the rope; once at the top he told me about the bathroom fittings. The designs I showed him later in the safety of his Birmingham office were a series of rough sketches which established the general concept, simple and robust. Models were then produced and the first stage of the range was manufactured as die castings. Subsequently more designs have been added to the range. Currently it is made with a chrome plated finish or in a variety of colours achieved by a coating of epoxy resin.

Bathroom fittings.

SHETLAND ISLES 1984

This survey of the dual roles of hand and machine ends with a project that has its origins in the very first days of my workshop. It combined hand work and machine production, but was brought into being, not through a design requirement, but through a totally different brief, to save jobs in the Shetlands and, if possible, to create more. The origins of this project date back even further than the opening of my workshop, and concern Donald McFall, a fellow silver student at Birmingham College of Art.

At college we were close friends and we travelled together through France, Switzerland and Italy on a motor-bike, Donald riding pillion all the way, a feat of bravery and endurance that still makes

me wonder. During our travels we studied examples of jewellery and silversmithing; this was in 1952 and little progress had been made in these countries with regard to design, but as there was a small travelling scholarship to spend, this seemed as good a trip as any to make.

Later, when I decided to open the workshop in Campden, Donald was convalescing from a major operation and it was generally agreed that he should leave Birmingham and take some country air in Campden. It was hardly a convalescence; the work was hard and the living conditions rough, but this toughening up did him good. For well over a year he was in the workshop, sometimes making his own work, sometimes helping me. He combined this

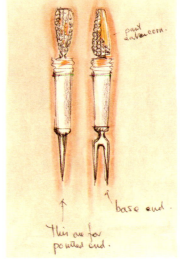

Sketch of corn on the cob eaters.

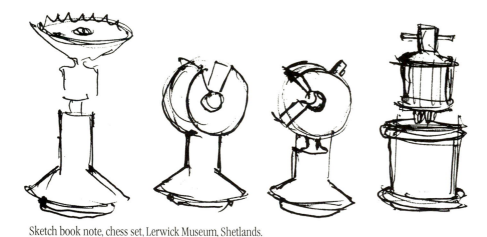

Sketch book note, chess set, Lerwick Museum, Shetlands.

with some teaching in Birmingham, and for a time this way of life worked well, until he was able to find a more lucrative consultancy post elsewhere; he left my workshop in 1956.

It was not until 1984 that he re-appeared in Campden, now Head of Development Services for Highland Craftpoint based in Beauly, Inverness-shire. He had fascinating stories to tell of his work in the remote areas of the Highlands and Islands, trying to maintain the living standards of the numerous and scattered craftsmen. The particular project which he wished to discuss with me concerned a jewellery business in the Shetlands, founded in 1954, which like many small craft workshops making batch production lines had experienced various changes of fortune.

The great oil boom had taken business to unprecedented heights, but now that was over, and the market had contracted; the workshop was losing money to the extent that if something was not done quickly it would close and

Serving pieces to be made in the Shetlands, ink and sepia wash.

eight jobs would be lost; that number in the Shetland Isles is a serious matter.

The problem was to harness the skills of lost wax casting in silver. The craftsmen were working for a market that scarcely existed, using a repertoire of designs based mainly on local motifs and Norse mythology; there were strong overtones of Scottish and Shetlands tradition, and this kind of thing did not travel very successfully to markets that knew nothing of the Shetland Isles.

In the summer of 1984 I made a trip to the Shetlands, combining it with a family holiday. In Lerwick there is a fine museum, and I spent some time making notes and sketches. Mr. Rae, the founder of the jewellery company, had told me about the museum and said, "I assure you I have examined all the historic motifs most carefully and anything worthwhile has already been made into jewellery." But there was one thing there that gave me an idea, a chess set carved from cotton reels by a sailor on a fishing boat; each reel was treated in a splendid and original way, but because of the discipline of the original shape the forms were all beautifully related and still recognisable as cotton reels.

This suggested to me the idea of making beautiful finials in the Shetlands, all related to a common base and theme; like the carved cotton reels they would be useful articles, attached to spoons and servers of all sorts, probably made in stainless steel elsewhere, while the Shetland work would be cast in large volumes in bronze and gilt, and the complete assembly, polishing and packaging undertaken in the workshop. It remained to draw the picture together. Harrison Fisher agreed to make the stainless steel components; a distributor agreed to sell the collection. Samples were made in Campden by John Limbrey before detailed development work was undertaken at the workshops of Highland Craftpoint.

It was an interesting approach, as it allowed great freedom of interpretation for the modellers at Beauly and the Shetlands, and it got away from some of the folksiness of the earlier work.

The year was 1958, the big project in the workshop was the tableware for the S.S. ORIANA, and I was working alone, deeply involved in the preparation of models and drawings.

Very few visitors found their way up the rickety stairs to the top of the old Silk Mill where I still have my workshop. It was a matter of surprise, therefore, when I heard a knock on my door, and even greater surprise when I greeted John Limbrey, a young silversmith who had studied with me in the School of Silversmithing at Birmingham College of Art, under Ralph Baxendale and Cyril Shiner.

After completing his National Service he had taken a post as a trainee silversmith with Robert Stone in London who was a fine craftsman specialising in ecclesiastical silverware. When John saw my workshop he said, "What a nice place to work, do you want any help?" In the shortest possible time, after settling his affairs with Robert Stone, John was working in Campden. Immediately he was engaged in the development of models for the Orient Line and he showed an instant understanding and appreciation of the problems involved in the designing and developing of products which are to be mass produced, in addition to commanding a superlative standard of craftsmanship in hand-made silverware.

That was 26 years ago, and we still work closely together with a feeling of complete understanding between us. John's contribution to the majority of the pieces illustrated in this book can be judged by the fact that he has made all the commissioned and ecclesiastical silverware since 1958, the majority of the domestic silver items, models in all manner of materials and production drawings of the majority of articles illustrated under the heading of MACHINE DESIGN.

John is also a talented watercolour artist, specialising in Cotswold scenes and in this area he enjoys a considerable following, his work being sought after by collectors.

There can be no doubt that two people working in close harmony and understanding can more than match the creative output of larger units. We observe a steady disciplined use of time, regular hours through success and failure.

Looking out of the windows there are fine views of Chipping Campden and the surrounding country-side and the rhythm of work continues to flow.